Build Deeper: Deep Learning Beginners' Guide

By Thimira Amaratunga

Build Deeper: Deep Learning Beginners' Guide

By Thimira Amaratunga

www.CodesOfInterest.com

First Edition

ISBN: 978-1549681066

Table of Contents

Preface

Deep Learning has become a household name. It's the new frontier in Artificial Intelligence. All the tech giants – Google, Facebook, Amazon, Microsoft, Apple, IBM and many more – are pursuing the goal, along with companies with the core focus on AI – DeepMind, OpenAI, Baidu, etc. – and thousands of start-ups following. Breakthroughs of Deep Learning seems to be happening daily, and the tech community is enthusiastically following the news.

With the advancement of the technologies behind it and the hype in the field, wouldn't you like to get into Deep Learning as well?

You might be thinking like "Deep learning is a vast and complicated field", "it's bleeding-edge, so there's not many resources", or "You need to learn a lot of complicated core concepts before you can start building Deep Learning systems". But, those really doesn't need to hold you back.

Deep Learning is vast: True. But it's built upon some beautiful natural and practical concepts you can get to know fairly quickly. If you keep thinking that you need to figure out all the theory behind it before you start to code, then you might never actually learn it. Sometimes the best way to learn is by actually trying it out. That's what this book is all about.

What this book covers

We'll be learning what Deep Learning is, and how it came to be. We'll look at some confusion and misconceptions regarding Deep Learning, and how to unravel the confusion. We'll then see the major milestones of Deep Learning throughout the years and their implications.

Next, we'll focus on what are the available technologies, tools, and resources that would help you get started. We'll then go through setting them up step-by-step, and we'll build our first Deep Learning program on top of them. Finally, we'll look back at what we learned, and a few ideas that you can try out next.

Who is this book for?

Enthusiasts of AI and Machine Learning, who would like to jump in and learn Deep Learning in a hands-on, and practical way. Those who like to learn by trying out, and actually coding. Those who aren't afraid to get their hands dirty with code.

This book is for the beginners for the Deep Learning field. We will be taking a more step-by-step approach focussed on code. If you're looking for more theoretical and conceptual aspects of Deep Learning, then this is not the book for you. While we cover some concepts behind Deep Learning, this book is more about how to get you quickly into coding.

What you need to follow this book

A computer to run code, and a good enthusiasm, with a bit of basic programming knowledge. That's all you need.

We'll be setting up everything else we need as we go through the book.

Sample Code, Diagrams, and Reference Links

The sample code we discuss in this book, high resolution colour images of the diagrams, and the reference links can be accessed from the following page:

http://www.codesofinterest.com/p/build-deeper.html

Questions and Feedback

Feedback is always welcome. Tell us what you likes, and what you disliked about this book. Your ideas on how to improve this are highly appreciated.

Nothing is error-free. So, if you spot an error in this book, please let us know. Your feedback will help us make this better for everyone.

You can contact us at: thimira@codesofinterest.com

Chapter 1 : What is Deep Learning?

Welcome to Deep Learning. You might be coming from a traditional computer science background learning about AI and Machine Learning. You could have been in the field of Artificial Intelligence for many years, or maybe just now getting your feet wet in the field. Or, you could be a technology enthusiast diving into the latest technology trends. In any of those cases, the first confusion you might confront is the multitude of terms such as "Artificial Intelligence", "Machine Learning", and "Deep Learning".

Figure 1-1: The confusion of Deep Learning

In recent times, the term Deep Learning seems to be the trend, so much so that it is now associated with some of the consumer technologies as well. Tech giants like Google, Apple, Amazon, Microsoft, IBM, and specialized companies for AI like DeepMind, OpenAI, Baidu, and many others are talking more and more about Deep Learning. You might be trying to figure out what each of these terms – Artificial Intelligence, Machine Learning, Deep Learning – mean, how they relate to each other, or whether these can be used interchangeably, and most importantly, how each of them came to be.

These are common questions when we first start getting into Deep Learning.

So, what is "Deep Learning"?

It's a subset of Machine Learning that deals with Hierarchical Feature Learning.

Ok, so, what is "Machine Learning"?

It's an approach to Artificial Intelligence which aims at providing machines with the ability to learn without explicitly programming.

Well then, what is "Artificial Intelligence"?

We should probably start from the beginning.

1.1 Intelligent Machines

Intelligent Machines is the idea that machines can be built that has intelligence parallel (or greater) to that of a human, giving them capability to perform tasks that requires human intelligence to perform.

Humans have been obsessed with this idea since ancient times, and written records of it can be traced back to 1300's (from the works of Ramon Llull, 1232 - 1315). By the 16th century, Gottfried Leibniz expanded on the idea with his **Calculus Ratiocinator** – a theoretical universal logical calculation framework. By the 19th century, the concept of "**Formal Reasoning**" has begun – with the introduction of the concepts such as "**Propositional Logic**" by George Boole, and "**Predicate Calculus**" by Gottlob Frege.

However, there was no formal research concept for AI, until the Dartmouth Conference in 1956.

1.2 Artificial Intelligence

In June 1956, many experts of the field – scientists and mathematicians – came together at the Dartmouth College (New Hampshire, US). This conference – titled The *Dartmouth Summer Research Project on Artificial Intelligence* – was the starting point of the formal research field of Artificial Intelligence. Allen Newell, Herbert A. Simon and Cliff Shaw – attendees of the conference – are the ones who built what is considered as the first Artificial Intelligence program – **The Logic Theorist** – which mimicked the logic problem solving of a human.

By 1960's, the AI research was in full swing. It had funding from the US Department of Defence, more and more AI research labs were being established, and the researchers were optimistic. Herbert A. Simon has predicted in 1965 that "Machines will be capable, within twenty years, of doing any work a man can do." (The Shape of Automation for Men and Management. New York: Harper & Row, 1965).

But, AI's didn't progress quite that fast.

Around the late 1990s and early 2000s, the researchers identified a problem in their approach to AI.

The problem?

In order to artificially create a machine with an intelligence, *one must first need to understand how intelligence work*.

But even today, we do not have a complete definition of what we call "intelligence".

In order to tackle the problem, the researchers decided to go ground-up – rather than trying to build an intelligence, they could look into building a system that can grow its own intelligence.

This idea created the new sub-field of AI called **Machine Learning**.

1.3   Machine Learning

Machine Learning is a subset of Artificial Intelligence which aims at providing machines with the ability to learn without explicitly programming. The idea is that such machines (or computer programs) once built will be able to evolve and adapt when they are exposed to new data.

The main idea behind Machine Learning is the ability of a learner to generalize from its experience. The learner (or the program), once given a set of training cases, must be able to build a generalized model upon them, which would allow it to decide upon new cases with sufficient accuracy.

Based on the approach, there are 3 learning methods of Machine Learning systems:

- **Supervised Learning** – the system is given a set of labelled cases (training set) and asked to create a generalized model on those to act on unseen cases.

- **Unsupervised Learning** – the system is given a set of cases unlabelled, and asked to find a pattern in them. Good for discovering hidden patterns.

- **Reinforcement Learning** – the system is asked to take an action, and is given a reward. The system must learn which actions would yield most rewards in certain situations.

With these techniques, the field of machine learning flourished. They were particularly successful in the areas of Computer Vision and Text Analysis.

Around 2010, few things happened that influenced Machine Learning research:

- More computing power became available. Evaluating more complex models became easier.

- Data processing and storage became cheaper. More data became available to consume.

- Our understanding of how the natural brain work increased. Allowing us to model new machine learning algorithms around them.

These breakthroughs propelled a new area of Machine Learning, called **Deep Learning**.

1.4 Deep Learning

Deep Learning is a subset of Machine Learning which focuses on an area of algorithms which was inspired by our understanding of how the brain works in order to obtain knowledge.

It's also referred to as Deep Structured Learning or Hierarchical Learning.

One of the definitions of Deep Learning is,

> "A sub-field within machine learning that is based on algorithms for learning multiple levels of representation in order to model complex relationships among data. Higher-level features and concepts are thus defined in terms of lower-level ones, and such a hierarchy of features is called a deep architecture" – Deep Learning: Methods and Applications.

Deep Learning builds upon the idea of Artificial Neural Networks and scales it up to be able to consume large amounts of data by deepening the networks in a very specific way. Through a deeper network a deep learning model has the capability of extracting features from raw data and "learn" about those features little-by-little in each layer, building up to the higher-level knowledge of the data. This technique is called **Hierarchical Feature Learning**, and it allows such systems to automatically learn complex features through multiple levels of abstraction with minimal human intervention.

> "The hierarchy of concepts allows the computer to learn complicated concepts by building them out of simpler ones. If we draw a graph showing how these concepts are built on top of each other, the graph is deep, with many layers. For this reason, we call this approach to AI deep learning." - Deep Learning. MIT Press, Ian Goodfellow and Yoshua Bengio and Aaron Courville.

One of the most distinct characteristics of Deep Learning – and one that made it quite popular and practical – is that it scales well, that is, the more data given to it, the better it performs. Unlike many older machine learning algorithms which has a higher bound to the amount of data they can ingest – often called a **"plateau in performance"** – Deep Learning models has no such limitations (theoretically) and they may be able to go beyond human comprehension. This is evident with the modern deep learning based image processing systems being able to outperform humans.

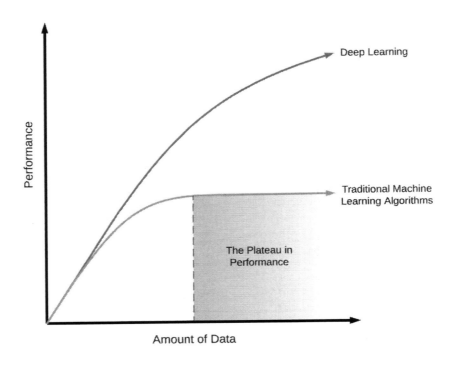

Figure 1-2: The lack of Plateau in Performance in Deep Learning

1.5 Convolutional Neural Networks

Convolutional Neural Networks are a prime example for Deep Learning. They were inspired by how the neurons are arranged in the visual cortex (the area of the brain which processes visual input). Here, not all neurons are connected to all of the inputs from the visual field. Instead, the visual field is 'tiled' with groups of neurons (called **Receptive fields**) which partially overlap each other.

Convolutional Neural Networks (CNNs) work in a similar way. They process in overlapping blocks of the input using mathematical convolution operators (which approximates how a receptive field works).

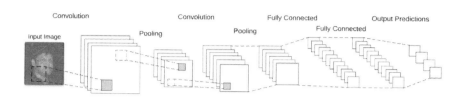

Figure 1-3: A Convolutional Neural Network

The first convolution layer uses a set of convolution filters to identify a set of low level features from the input image. These identified low level features are then pooled (from the pooling layers) and given as the input to the next convolution layer, which uses another set of convolution filters to identify a set of higher level features from the lower level features identified earlier. This continues for several layers, where each convolution layer uses the inputs from the previous layer to identify higher level features than the previous layer. Finally, the output of the last convolution layer is passed on to a set of fully-connected layers for the final classification.

1.6   How Deep?

With the capabilities of Deep Learning grasped, there's one question that usually comes up when one first learns about Deep Learning:

If we say that deeper and more complex models gives Deep Learning models the capabilities to surpass even human capabilities, then **how deep a machine learning model should be to be considered a Deep Learning model**?

It turns out, we were asking the wrong question. We need to look at Deep Learning from a different angle to understand it.

Let's take a step back and see how a Deep Learning model works. Let's take the Convolutional Neural Networks as the example again.

As mentioned above, the convolution filters of a CNN attempts to identify lower-level features first, and use those identified features to identify higher-level features gradually through multiple steps.

This is the Hierarchical Feature Learning we talked about earlier, and it is the key of Deep Learning, and what differentiates it from traditional Machine learning algorithms.

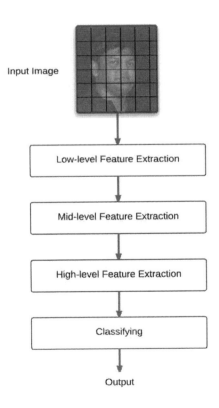

Figure 1-4: Hierarchical Feature Learning

A Deep Learning model (such as a Convolutional Neural Network) does not try to understand the entire problem at once. I.e. it does not try to grasp all the features of the input at once, as traditional algorithms tried to do. What it does is look at the input piece by piece, and derive lower level patterns/features from it. It then uses these lower level features to gradually identify higher level features, through many layers, hierarchically. This allows Deep Learning models to learn complicated patterns, by gradually building them up from simpler ones. This also allows Deep Learning models to comprehend the world better, and they not only 'see' the features, but also see the hierarchy of how those features are built upon.

And of course, having to learn features hierarchically means that the model must have many layers in it. Which means that such a model will be 'deep'.

That brings us back to our original question: It is not that we call deep models as Deep Learning. It is that in order to achieve hierarchical learning the models need to be deep. The deepness is a by-product of implementing Hierarchical Feature Learning.

So, how do we identify whether a model is a Deep Learning model or now?

Simply, if the model uses Hierarchical Feature Learning – identifying lower level features first, and then build upon them to identify higher level features (e.g. by using convolution filters) – then it is a Deep Learning model. If not, then no matter how many layers your model has then it's not considered a Deep Learning model. Which means that a neural network with a 100 fully-connected layers (and only fully-connected layers) wouldn't be a Deep Learning model, but a network with a handful of convolutional layers would be.

1.7   Is Deep Learning just CNNs?

When we talk about deep Learning, we talk about Convolutional Neural Networks (CNNs) a lot. And, you might be wondering whether Deep Learning is just CNNs.

No.

Actually, all of the following models are considered Deep Learning.

- Convolutional Neural Networks
- Deep Boltzmann Machine
- Deep Belief Networks
- Stacked Autoencoders

But, CNNs are the most 'defined' – and addressing more relatable problem spaces – in the Deep Learning field, at least at the moment. But, keep in mind that CNNs are not the whole picture of Deep Learning.

1.8   How does it all come together?

So, getting back at our original questions:

How does the areas of Artificial Intelligence, Machine Learning and Deep Learning relate to each other?

Simply put, Machine Learning is a subset (an approach) of Artificial Intelligence, and Deep Learning is a subset of Machine Learning, all working towards the common goal of creating an intelligent machine.

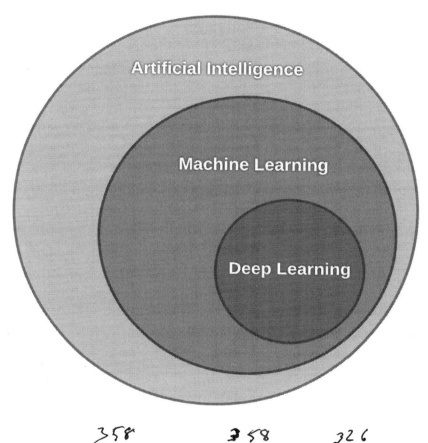

358   3 58   32 6

Figure 1-5: How Artificial Intelligence, Machine Learning, and Deep Learning relates to each other

And here's a quick look back at how Deep Learning, Machine Learning, and Artificial Intelligence evolved through the years,

761   *Il indrive every sees Eoshafid

meseye °

2 7b°

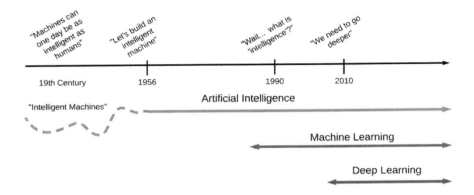

Figure 1-6: The evolution of Deep Learning

With the capabilities demonstrated and the success achieved by Deep Learning, we may be a step closer to the ultimate goal of Artificial Intelligence – building a machine with a human level (or greater) intelligence.

Chapter 2 : Milestones of Deep Learning

Deep Learning has been around for about a decade now. Since its inception, Deep Learning has taken the world by storm due to its success. Here are some of the more significant achievements of Deep Learning throughout the years.

2.1   AlexNet – 2012

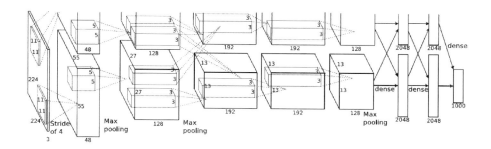

Figure 2-1: The AlexNet Architecture (Source: Research Paper)

AlexNet marked the start of an era, by bringing the success of Deep Learning to the mainstream.

- Proved that Convolutional Neural Networks actually works. AlexNet – and its research paper "ImageNet Classification with Deep Convolutional Neural Networks" by Alex Krizhevsky, Ilya Sutskever, and Geoffrey E. Hinton – is commonly considered as what brought Deep Learning in to the mainstream.

- Won 2012 ILSVRC (ImageNet Large-Scale Visual Recognition Challenge) with 15.4% error rate. (For reference, the 2nd best entry at ILSVRC had 26.2% error rate).

- 8 layers: 5 convolutional, 3 fully connected.

- Used ReLU for the non-linearity function rather than the conventional tanh function used until then.

- Introduced the use of Dropout Layers, and Data Augmentation to overcome overfitting.

Research Paper: **"ImageNet Classification with Deep Convolutional Neural Networks"** – Alex Krizhevsky, Ilya Sutskever, Geoffrey E. Hinton.

2.2   ZF Net – 2013

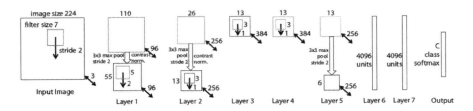

Figure 2-2: The ZF Net Architecture (Source: Research Paper)

16

With AlexNet starting the trend, ZF Net kept it going. While continuing the success of AlexNet, the ZF net attempted to answer why convolutional neural networks perform so well.

- Winner of ILSVRC 2013 with an error rate of 11.2%.
- Similar to the AlexNet architecture, with some tweaks and fine tuning to improve the performance.
- Introduced the Deconvolutional Network (a.k.a. DeConvNet), a visualization technique to view the inner workings of a CNN, which allowed understanding why CNNs perform well.

The Deconvolutional technique is still used today to view how the internal convolutions perform in a network.

Research Paper: "Visualizing and Understanding Convolutional Networks" – Matthew D. Zeiler, Rob Fergus.

2.3   VGG Net – 2014

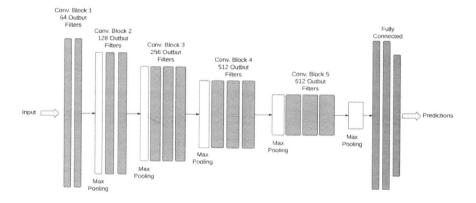

Figure 2-3: The VGG Net Architecture

Note: Larger diagram of the network is available at the Appendix I.

17

One of the most popular Deep Learning architectures, due to its simplicity.

- Won the "Classification + localization" category of the ILSVRC 2014 (Not the overall winner), with an error rate of 7.3%.
- The VGG architecture worked well with both image classification and localization.
- Has 2 variations: VGG16 (16 layers), and VGG19 (19 layers)
- Uses 3x3 filters. (Compared to 11x11 filters of AlexNet, and 7x7 filters of ZF Net).
- Proved that simple deep structures works for hierarchical feature extraction.

The VGG Net architectures are still popular, as they are easy to construct and the training time is less compared to more complex models. They are good candidates for experimenting with transfer learning.

Research Paper: "Very Deep Convolutional Networks for Large-scale Image Recognition" – Karen Simonyan, Andrew Zisserman.

2.4 GoogLeNet – 2014/2015

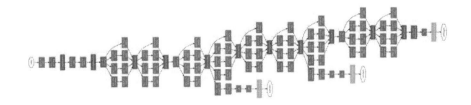

Figure 2-4: The GoogLeNet Architecture (Source: Research Paper)

Note: Larger diagram of the network is available at the Appendix I.

18

This is where Deep Learning became creative, in terms of the network architectures. The authors of GoogLeNet introduced a unique architecture in order to increase the computational efficiency, which broke the idea that deep learning models need to always be sequential.

- GoogLeNet was the winner of ILSVRC 2014 with an error rate of 6.7%.

- Introduced the Inception Module, which emphasized that the layers of a CNN doesn't always need to be stacked up sequentially.

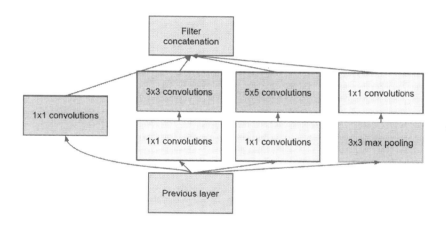

Figure 2-5: The Inception Module (Source: Research Paper)

- 22 blocks of layers (over 100 layers when considered individually).

- No fully connected layers.

- Proved that optimized non-sequential structures may work better than sequential ones.

While the original architecture was named GoogLeNet, two improved models were releases subsequently which were named **Inception V2**, and **Inception V3**.

Research Paper: "**Going Deeper with Convolutions**" – Christian Szegedy, Wei Liu, Yangqing Jia, Pierre Sermanet, Scott Reed, Dragomir Anguelov, Dumitru Erhan, Vincent Vanhoucke, Andrew Rabinovich, Google Inc., University of North Carolina, Chapel Hill, University of Michigan, Ann Arbor, Magic Leap Inc.

2.5   Microsoft ResNet – 2015

Figure 2-6: The ResNet Architecture (Source: Research Paper)

Note: Larger diagram of the network is available at the Appendix I.

Typically, if you keep adding layers sequentially to a model, they tend to get worse after a certain point, as the model will start to overfit. ResNet was an attempt to overcome this limitation by introducing the 'Residual Block', which resulted in an impressively deep network, with an even impressive accuracy.

- The ResNet50 won ILSVRC 2015.
- With an error rate of 3.6%, the ResNet has a higher accuracy than a human (A typical human is said to have an error rate of about 5-10%).

- Ultra-deep (quoting the authors) architecture with 152 layers.
- Introduced the Residual Block, to reduce overfitting. (Which gave the name to the network "Residual Network", a.k.a. ResNet).

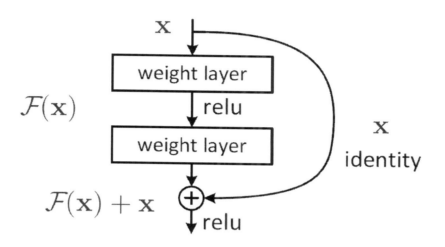

Figure 2-7: The Residual Block (Source: Research Paper)

The ResNet architecture has been proven to be scalable. There has been successful attempts to increase up to 1000 layers. (See the References section)

Research Paper: **"Deep Residual Learning for Image Recognition"** – Kaiming He, Xiangyu Zhang, Shaoqing Ren, Jian Sun, Microsoft Research.

2.6　What is the ILSVRC?

The **ImageNet Large Scale Visual Recognition Challenge** (ILSVRC) is the annual Computer Vision challenge conducted by the ImageNet project. The ImageNet project was started around 2007, with the intension of providing a complete and easily accessible image database for Visual Object Recognition research. ImageNet organises the images based on **WordNet** – a lexical database for the English language, which groups English words into sets of synonyms called **synsets**. The ImageNet project aims at providing at least 1000 images for each synset, and has about ten million images as of now, all of which are hand-annotated and with bounding boxes.

The ILSVRC is held annually by the ImageNet project, where institutions and research groups both from the industry and academia compete against each other with their Machine Learning and Computer Vision algorithms. The task is to correctly classify over 100,000 images in to 1000 categories, with a training set of about a million labelled images. The objective of the competition is to allow the competitors to measure and compare their applications and algorithms. A secondary objective is to measure and document the progress of Machine Learning for Computer Vision at a higher level over the years.

2.7 Why Computer Vision?

Looking back at our list of the milestones in Deep Learning, you'll notice that all of those projects deals with Computer Vision. Even the ImageNet competitions focus on visual recognition.

Why is that?

Does Deep Learning only work on Computer Vision?

Not really.

Vision – understanding and giving a meaning to visual inputs – is something humans are exceptionally good at. Ability to understand the surroundings is considered a sign of intelligence. So, when it comes to building intelligent machines, vision is one of the core capabilities that we wish an intelligent machine would possess. And, it's easy to validate, since we can easily compare it with the ability of a human.

Therefore, exploring vision capabilities has become a core area in Deep Learning research.

The achievements deep learning gather in the vision field may shape how we approach other fields as well. Thanks to the capability of 'Transfer learning' (which we'll discuss in a later chapter) deep learning is able to apply knowledge gained from one domain to a different domain. While typically this capability is used to apply knowledge from one vision model to another, it is speculated – and many research are ongoing – on how the knowledge from a model trained on visual input may apply to a non-visual context.

Chapter 3 :   Where to Start Your Deep Learning

Now that we know what Deep Learning is, and what it's capable, you might be eager to build one of your own Deep Learning models.

So, what do we need to start?

You need to select a programming language to write your code, and select from a couple of deep learning frameworks for that language, throw in a selection of utility libraries and tools to help you, and then just start coding.

3.1   Programming Language – Python

You might be thinking "why Python"?

Is it the only language for Deep Learning? Definitely no.

When you understand the concepts, you could use pretty much any language to implement deep learning. But, some languages have already established tool, libraries, and frameworks for supporting machine learning and deep learning tasks. In order to avoid re-inventing already existing stuff, we choose a language that has a lot of such pre-existing support.

So, is Python the best language for Deep Learning? That's a tricky question.

Figure 3-1: The Python Logo

When we look for the most popular languages for machine learning, a couple of languages stands out: Python, R, C++, C, MATLAB. Each of them has their own advantages and disadvantages.

We choose Python because of couple of points, especially when you are starting to learn deep learning.

For a beginner for deep learning – especially someone already having a programming background – writing code in Python would be more natural. You get to use most of the familiar object oriented and functional programming concepts. While not having as good performance as C or C++, Python is still pretty fast. Having the capability to run the code on multiple CPUs and GPUs helps a lot too. And, most C/C++ libraries tend to have Python interfaces as well (e.g. OpenCV, Dlib, Caffe, etc.). Compared to R and MATLAB, the availability of deep learning and machine learning libraries as similar in Python. But considering the maturity of the libraries, Python libraries seems to be the more bleeding edge. Most of the latest deep learning frameworks are being developed for Python (e.g. TensorFlow).

One of the biggest advantages of using Python is the deploy-ability. Say, you build an awesome deep learning program, and you want to deploy it as a web service. With Python, it's fairly straightforward. With R, MATLAB or C/C++, it'll take quite a bit of effort.

Considering all these benefits, we're going to use Python for our deep learning experiments.

3.2   Package and Environment Management – Anaconda

Anaconda is an Open Source platform of Python and R languages, meant for machine learning, data science, large-scale data processing, and scientific computing. Anaconda contains optimized versions of Python for many platforms and architectures.

Figure 3-2: The Anaconda Logo

It's not only just a Python distribution, it's also a package, dependency, and environment manager for Python. Through its **conda** package manager, Anaconda allows easy creation of virtual isolated environments – with its own Python binaries and packages – to experiment with. You can create multiple independent Python environments of multiple Python versions, and their own independent installed packages, based on your needs.

Anaconda also contains hundreds of pre-built and tested packages for machine learning, scientific computing, and data processing, which you can directly install through the conda package manager. It removes the hassle of finding, building, installing, and dependency managing of packages and libraries.

3.3   Utility Libraries in Python

When working with Python, and the Deep Learning frameworks (which, we'll be looking at in a bit), having the following set of utility libraries will make a lot of tasks easier.

- **NumPy** – Adds the support to handle large multi-dimensional arrays in Python, along with a collection of high-level mathematical functions that can be applies across arrays.
- **SciPy** – The scientific cousin of NumPy. SciPy adds support for mathematical optimization, linear algebra, integral and differential equations, interpolation, special functions, Fourier transform, and signal processing to Python.

- **Pillow** – Pillow is a fork of PIL (Python Image Library), which adds image processing capabilities to Python. It adds extensive file format support for images, with efficient internal representation mechanisms.

- **Scikit-Image** – Adds a set of higher-level image processing capabilities to Python, such as edge detection, equalization, feature detection, and segmentation.

- **h5py** – Adds the support of HDF5 binary data format to Python. The HDF5 format is used in many of the Machine Learning frameworks as it allows easy storage and handling of large – terabyte level – data as if they were internal data arrays.

- **Matplotlib** – Matplotlib is a sophisticated 2D plotting and data visualization library for Python, allowing you to create publication quality plots and figures on a variety of platforms.

Apart from the above, if you're installing on Windows, it's better to have to following two packages also, which aids in installing some of the packages with Anaconda.

- mingw
- libpython

3.4 Deep Learning Frameworks

3.4.1 TensorFlow

TensorFlow is the 2nd generation Machine Learning library by the Google Brain Team, and has gained huge popularity in recent times due to its Deep Learning capabilities. First released on November, 2015, as the successor of **DistBelief** (Google Brains 1st generation library), TensorFlow initially had only support for Python on Linux. Since then, TensorFlow has added support to Java and Go, and now works on Windows and Mac OS natively. TensorFlow is capable of running on either CPU or GPU (With NVIDIA CUDA), and works on lower end devices like mobile phones – on Android and iOS – and Raspberry Pi devices.

Figure 3-3: The TensorFlow Logo

29

TensorFlow uses stateful data flow graphs for its numerical calculations, where the nodes of the graph represents mathematical operations, while the edges of the graph represents the data that flows through the nodes. The data is represented as multidimensional arrays (tensors), hence the name 'TensorFlow'.

On February, 2017, TensorFlow released version 1.0, and is currently on version 1.3 (as of August 2017). It's one of the most actively developed Machine Learning libraries out there.

3.4.2 Theano

Theano is a machine learning and numerical computation library, developed by the researchers at the University of Montreal. The idea behind Theano is to allow developer to write symbolic expressions, which it then dynamically compiles on to run on various architectures. The dynamic C code generation feature of Theano allows programs to efficiently run, and take advantages of, different CPU or GPU architectures. Theano has a tight integration with NumPy, which it use to represent its multidimensional data structures.

Figure 3-4: The Theano Logo

Theano has been in active development since 2007, and is considered an alternative to TensorFlow as both supports similar features.

3.4.3 Keras

Keras is a higher-level neural networks library for Python, which is capable of running on top of **TensorFlow**, **CNTK** (Microsoft Cognitive Toolkit), or **Theano**, (and with limited support for **MXNet** and **Deeplearning4j**). The focus on Keras is to allow fast experimentation and prototyping of code, by being user friendly, minimal, modular and extensible. Keras gives you more cleaner and structured code than using the backend libraries directly.

Figure 3-5: The Keras Logo

Keras supports convolutional networks and recurrent networks, as well as combinations of the two, and can run on both CPU and GPU based on the capabilities of the backend being used.

With the release of TensorFlow v1.0 in February 2017, the TensorFlow team is adding dedicated support to Keras in the TensorFlow library.

3.4.4 Scikit-Learn

Figure 3-6: The Scikit-Learn Logo

Scikit-Learn (formerly scikits.learn) is a library for machine learning, data mining, and data analytics. It gives capabilities such as classification, regression, clustering, dimensionality reduction, model selection, and preprocessing (feature extraction and normalization). Scikit-Learn has one of the best collection of machine learning and utility algorithms for data processing.

3.5 Computer Vision Libraries

Why do we need computer vision libraries? As we discussed in the previous chapter, when working with Deep Learning, you'll run in to quite a lot of tasks requiring computer vision and image processing. So, having these libraries would make things easier.

3.5.1 OpenCV

OpenCV (Open Source Computer Vision) is the de-facto standard library when it comes to computer vision. Aimed at real-time computer vision applications, OpenCV is loaded with vision and image processing algorithms. It also has built-in limited machine learning functions to aid with building applications for computer vision.

Figure 3-7: The OpenCV Logo

Originally developed by Intel, and initially released on June, 2000, OpenCV has since been made open source, and is now released under the BSD license. Primarily written in C/C++, it had interfaces for C, C++, Python, and Java. It can be run on Windows, Linux, Mac OS, iOS and Android.

Currently, there's two major branches of OpenCV – v2.x and v3.x. The 3.x branch contains the latest development and is the one more optimized.

3.5.2 Dlib

Dlib in not just a computer vision library. It's a library and a toolkit for machine learning, linear algebra, data structures, image processing, computer vision, data mining, XML and text parsing, numerical optimization, and many other tasks, which happens to have some handy functions for computer vision also.

Figure 3-8: The Dlib Logo

Dlib has some of the most optimized out-of-the-box face detection and face landmark detection models available. It also has easy to use function to train your own object detectors and shape predictors.

3.6 Optimizers

Optimizers are libraries and tools which helps to run your code faster. Most optimizer tools work by giving your code direct access to the capabilities of the hardware of the system.

3.6.1 CUDA and cuDNN

Figure 3-9: The NVIDIA CUDA Logo

CUDA is a parallel computing platform and programming model invented by NVIDIA. It enables dramatic increases in computing performance by harnessing the power of the GPU. cuDNN - or, CUDA Deep Neural Network library - is a GPU-accelerated library of primitives for deep neural networks. cuDNN provides highly tuned implementations for standard routines such as forward and backward convolution, pooling, normalization, and activation layers. Using CUDA and cuDNN along with either Theano or TensorFlow could extremely speed up your neural networks (networks which took hours to train might take just minutes). The only requirement is that you need to have a CUDA supported NVIDIA GPU in your system.

3.6.2 OpenBLAS

OpenBLAS is an open source implementation of the BLAS (**Basic Linear Algebra Subprograms**), containing optimizations for many specific processor types. Machine Learning libraries such as Theano is able to speed up certain routines by utilizing BLAS libraries. You will see a noticeable speed difference when running your models with OpenBLAS on CPU. However, some libraries, such as TensorFlow, have their own internal optimizers, so will not see any improvements with OpenBLAS.

Now that we know what tools are available for us to get started with Deep Learning, let's start setting them up.

Chapter 4 :   How to Set Them Up

So, now that we know what we need to get started, let's start setting them up.

We'll be using Anaconda Python as the Python distribution as well as the package manager because of the advantages we discussed in the last chapter. Since we have to mix both the **conda** package manager and **pip** to get all the packages we need, the order of which we install is a little bit important. So, we would recommend the following order.

1. Anaconda Python
2. Packages from conda
3. OpenCV
4. Dlib
5. Theano
6. Keras
7. TensorFlow

For installing CUDA and/or OpenBLAS. The order doesn't really matter, as long as you have them installed by the time you first run Keras, TensorFlow, or Theano.

When using both the conda package manager and pip (default Python package manager), it's better to give priority to conda first. Only use pip to install if you can't find a conda package for the package you're trying to install.

4.1   Anaconda Python

Installing Anaconda is fairly straightforward. You just need to head over to the Anaconda Downloads page (https://www.continuum.io/downloads) and download the appropriate installer package for the platform (Windows, Mac OS, or Linux) and the architecture (32-Bit or 64-Bit) of your system.

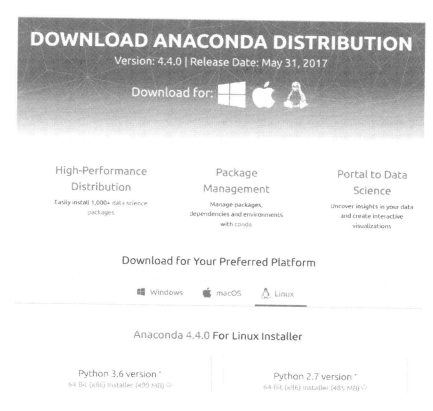

Figure 4-1: The Anaconda Downloads page

Installing is as simple as running the downloaded installer in Windows or Mac OS. In Linux, you can install it by running,

```
bash /path/to/downloaded/Anaconda3-<version>-
Linux-<architecture>.sh
```

e.g.

```
bash ~/Downloads/Anaconda3-4.4.0-Linux-
x86_64.sh
```

Remember to include the 'bash' in the command, even if you are not running it on a Bash shell.

We recommend using **Python 3.5 64-Bit** for your deep learning experiments, as that version would give least compatibility issues, and give the best performance (compared to the Python 2.7 branch). You will notice that the Anaconda installer comes with Python 3.6 (or newer) as default. That not a problem, as you can create anaconda environments with different Python versions. You can specify which Python version to use when creating the environment.

4.2   Conda Environment and Libraries

After Anaconda is installed, it's recommended to go through the "Anaconda Test Drive" - https://conda.io/docs/test-drive.html. It's a tutorial – which should take you less than 30 minutes – that walks you through the commands and the capabilities of Anaconda.

Once you get a hang of 'conda', it's time to create the conda environment and install the necessary packages.

With conda, we can install the initial list of packages at the same time we create the environment. So, we can basically run the following,

```
conda create --name deep-learning python=3.5
numpy scipy scikit-learn scikit-image pillow
h5py matplotlib
```

--name deep-learning – We set the name of the environment to be 'deep-learning'. You can change that to anything you like.

python=3.5 – We tell conda to create the new environment with Python 3.5

These parameters are followed by the list of package names to install in the environment.

Note: On Windows, you should add two more packages – 'mingw' and 'libpython'. So the create command should be,

```
conda create --name deep-learning python=3.5
numpy scipy scikit-learn scikit-image pillow
h5py matplotlib mingw libpython
```

Once the environment is created (which will take few minutes to get everything installed), you can activate it.

On Linux or Mac OS run,

```
source activate deep-learning
```

On Windows, it's simply,

```
activate deep-learning
```

4.3   OpenCV

OpenCV has pre-built binaries for Windows. For other platforms, you will need to build it from the source. Even with the Windows pre-built binaries from the official site, you will have issues with getting it to work on Python 3.5 64-Bit.

So, the next option is to check whether there's a conda package for OpenCV.

There's no OpenCV package in the official Anaconda package list. But no need to fear, because in the Anaconda community repository – the Anaconda Cloud – there are hundreds of packages available, created by the community. The group Conda-Forge has created a package for OpenCV 3.2 which works on Windows, Linux, or Mac OS, on both 32-bit and 64-Bit. We can install it simply by using,

```
conda install -c conda-forge opencv=3.2.0
```

This is currently the easiest way to get OpenCV on any platform.

If you do like to give an attempt on building OpenCV from source, you can follow the handy guide we've created on "**Installing OpenCV from source on Anaconda Python on Ubuntu**" at the following link:

http://www.codesofinterest.com/2017/01/installing-opencv-source-ubuntu.html

(Please note that some of the package names might have changed in newer Linux versions).

4.4   Dlib

If you go through the instructions to install the Dlib Python interface from the official website (http://dlib.net), it will say to install it with just 'pip install dlib', provided that the dependencies are already installed. What it doesn't really say is how hard it is to get the dependencies – Cmake and Boost-Python – installed in certain systems.

So, again, Anaconda comes to our rescue. Conda-Forge has a package for Dlib 19.4 also. We just need to run,

```
conda install -c conda-forge dlib=19.4
```

Conda will ask to install a lot of dependant packages as it installs Dlib, and will usually upgrade/downgrade few of the already installed packages automatically to fix package version conflicts. So, just say 'yes' when prompted to install/update/downgrade a package, and conda will take care of the rest.

4.5   Theano

Theano is available through pip. You can install it using 'pip install theano'. But since Theano is developed actively, the version on PyPI is always older, and may not have the latest features. Therefore, it's better to always install the latest development version of Theano from Git,

```
pip install --upgrade --no-deps
git+git://github.com/Theano/Theano.git
```

Remember to always install Theano before you try to install Keras, as Keras will try to automatically install Theano if it doesn't find it already installed, which will result in an older version of Theano getting installed.

4.6   Keras

Keras is the easiest to install from all of the libraries we're using. It's available through pip, and can be installed using,

```
pip install keras
```

Once Keras is installed, you need to select which 'backend' to use with it. As we discussed in the last chapter, Keras works on top of either TensorFlow or Theano. It defaults to TensorFlow when first installed.

The Kesas settings – including which backend to use – is defined in the **keras.json** file, which is located at **~/.keras/keras.json** in Linux and Mac OS, and at **%USERPROFILE%\.keras\keras.json** on Windows.

The default keras.json file would look like this,

```
{

    "epsilon": 1e-07,

    "floatx": "float32",

    "image_data_format": "channels_last",

    "backend": "tensorflow"

}
```

The "backend" parameter should either be "tensorflow" or "theano". When switching the backend, make sure to switch the "image_data_format" parameter too. For "tensorflow" backend, it should be "channels_last". For "theano", it should be "channels_first".

Why is this important?

The image_data_format parameter affects how each of the backends treat the data dimensions when working with multi-dimensional convolution layers (such as Conv2D, Conv3D, Conv2DTranspose, Copping2D, ... and any other 2D or 3D layer). Specifically, it defines where the 'channels' dimension is in the input data.

Both TensorFlow and Theano expects a four dimensional tensor as input. But where TensorFlow expects the 'channels' dimension as the last dimension (index 3, where the first is index 0) of the tensor – i.e. tensor with shape (samples, rows, cols, channels) – Theano will expect 'channels' at the second dimension (index 1) – i.e. tensor with shape (samples, channels, rows, cols). The outputs of the convolutional layers will also follow this pattern.

So, the image_data_format parameter, once set in keras.json, will tell Keras which dimension ordering to use in its convolutional layers.

Mixing up the channels order would result in your models being trained in unexpected ways.

Other than by setting the parameter in keras.json you can manipulate it in the code as well. You can get and set the image_data_format through the keras.backend package.

To get the image_data_format, you can use the image_data_format() function,

```
from keras import backend as K
print(K.image_data_format())
```

To set the image_data_format, pass the string either 'channels_first' or 'channels_last' to set_image_data_format() function.

```
from keras import backend as K
K.set_image_data_format('channels_first')
```

You can also set it per layer, using the data_format parameter in the 2D and 3D convolutional layers.

```
model.add(Conv2D(20, (5, 5), padding="same",
input_shape=(height, width, depth),
data_format="channels_first"))
```

4.7 TensorFlow

Installing TensorFlow used to be a complicated task. Up until version r0.12, it only worked on Linux, and had very specific dependency list to be installed to work properly. After version r0.12, things got a bit easier, and got the Windows compatibility. And, with version 1.0, installing TensorFlow has become quite simple.

TensorFlow now can be installed on Linux, Mac OS and Windows. The choice you can make is to either go with the CPU version or the GPU version of TensorFlow. If you have a CUDA compatible NVIDIA GPU, then it's better to go with the GPU version. (We'll talk about getting CUDA installed in a bit). On some occasions, it's safe to install the CPU version first, as it'll give you less issues.

The next step is to head over to the official TensorFlow page, and get the Python package URL for Python 3.5 for your platform.

For the latest version (at the time of this writing) – version 1.3.0 – the URLs are as follows:

Linux

CPU

```
https://storage.googleapis.com/tensorflow/linu
x/cpu/tensorflow-1.3.0-cp35-cp35m-
linux_x86_64.whl
```

GPU

```
https://storage.googleapis.com/tensorflow/linu
x/gpu/tensorflow_gpu-1.3.0-cp35-cp35m-
linux_x86_64.whl
```

Windows

CPU

```
https://storage.googleapis.com/tensorflow/wind
ows/cpu/tensorflow-1.3.0-cp35-cp35m-
win_amd64.whl
```

GPU

```
https://storage.googleapis.com/tensorflow/wind
ows/gpu/tensorflow_gpu-1.3.0-cp35-cp35m-
win_amd64.whl
```

Mac OS

CPU

```
https://storage.googleapis.com/tensorflow/mac/
cpu/tensorflow-1.3.0-py3-none-any.whl
```

GPU

[There's no GPU version available for Mac OS for TensorFlow 1.3.*]

Once you have the URL, install it in the conda environment you created earlier by running the following two commands.

Note: You need to run both these commands. Installing it like this ensures there are no package dependency conflicts. The URL used for both the commands should be the same.

```
pip install --upgrade --no-deps
YourTensorFlowURL

pip install YourTensorFlowURL
```

Replace 'YourTensorFlowURL' with the actual URL from above you want to install.

E.g. To install the GPU version on Windows,

```
pip install --upgrade --no-deps
https://storage.googleapis.com/tensorflow/wind
ows/gpu/tensorflow_gpu-1.2.1-cp35-cp35m-
win_amd64.whl

pip install
https://storage.googleapis.com/tensorflow/wind
ows/gpu/tensorflow_gpu-1.2.1-cp35-cp35m-
win_amd64.whl
```

4.8 OpenBLAS (Optional)

Installing OpenBLAS is only needed if you're running Theano on CPU. TensorFlow has its own internal CPU optimizers, and thus doesn't need (or use) OpenBLAS. But with Theano, it's recommended to have OpenBLAS setup, as it sometimes doubles the speed of which deep learning models train on it.

On Linux, installing OpenBLAS can be done by running the following command,

```
sudo apt-get install libopenblas-dev
```

For Windows, OpenBLAS has pre-built binaries. You can get them from the official Sourceforge page:

https://sourceforge.net/projects/openblas/files/v0.2.15/

You need both the **OpenBLAS-v0.2.15-Win64-int32.zip** and the **mingw64_dll.zip** files, and extract them to a globally accessible folder, and add them to the Windows system path. You then need to edit the **.thenorc** file to point to the OpenBLAS binaries.

You can check the following article at Codes of Interest for the specific steps: **Getting Theano working with OpenBLAS on Windows** (http://www.codesofinterest.com/2016/10/getting-theano-working-with-openblas-on.html).

4.9   NVIDIA CUDA and cuDNN

The main requirement to get CUDA working is that you have a CUDA compatible NVIDIA GPU on your system. So, before starting to setup CUDA, make sure your GPU is compatible by checking with the official list of NVIDIA CUDA supported GPUs: https://developer.nvidia.com/cuda-gpus.

In order to get CUDA working, you need to have a C++ compiler installed. On Linux, this can be **GCC**. On Windows, you will need **Microsoft Visual Studio** installed. CUDA isn't compatible with the latest Visual Studio 2017 (at the time of this writing), so you will need to use **Visual Studio 2015**. The free community edition of VS 2015 will be sufficient.

You need to setup the following, in that order.

1. Microsoft Visual Studio 2015
2. CUDA 8.0
3. cuDNN 5.1 for CUDA 8.0 (Or, the latest version of cuDNN that supports CUDA 8.0)

Start by installing Visual Studio 2015. When you install, make sure to select 'Custom Installation', and select 'Visual C++' in the programming language selection (by default, C++ is not selected). Once installed, check whether you have C++ capability by checking the 'New Project' options.

Figure 4-2: Visual Studio 2015 Installed with C++ support

Once Visual Studio is installed, head over to NVIDIA CUDA
Downloads page - https://developer.nvidia.com/cuda-downloads - and
download CUDA 8.0 for your OS.

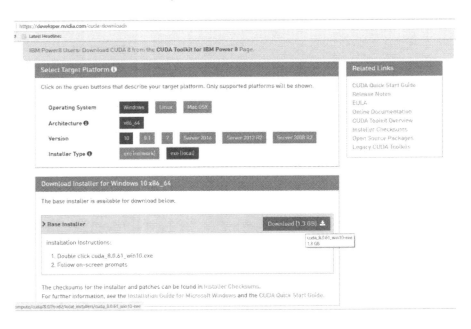

Figure 4-3: Downloading CUDA 8.0

You should also download cuDNN - https://developer.nvidia.com/cudnn. Downloading cuDNN requires you to create a free NVIDIA Developer account. There may be multiple versions of cuDNN available, so make sure to download the latest version compatible with the CUDA version you're using. E.g. "cuDNN 5.1 for CUDA 8.0".

Figure 4-4: Downloading cuDNN 5.1 for CUDA 8.0

Start by installing CUDA. If you go with the "Express Installation", and you already have the latest display driver installed, the installer will attempt to overwrite the already installed display driver (with an older version driver). So, if you already have the latest driver (and GeForce Experience installed), it's better to go in the "Custom Installation" path and deselect the GeForce Experience and Display Driver options.

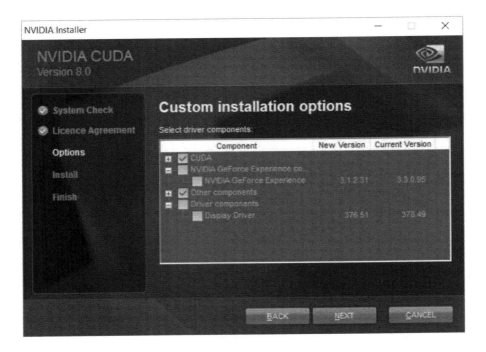

Figure 4-5: Custom install options of CUDA

You can keep the defaults for everything else in the CUDA installer.

cuDNN is not an installer. It's a Zip file, which you need to extract to the directory which CUDA was installed to. When you extract cuDNN, you get 3 directories: **'bin'**, **'include'**, and **'lib'**. Copy these to the corresponding directories of the CUDA install directory. I.e. The contents of cuDNN 'bin' go in to CUDA 'bin', and so on.

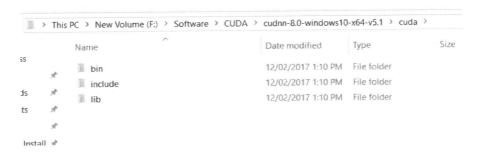

Figure 4-6: Extracting cuDNN

Once everything is copied, the CUDA and cuDNN is now ready for your deep learning models to run.

But, make sure to verify the installation as described in the next section.

4.10 Verify Installations

After you install all the required packages and libraries, it's best to do some preliminary checks to ensure that everything installed correctly. Otherwise, you'll run into issues later when running your code, and wouldn't know whether there's a bug in the code, or an issue with the installation.

Now, we won't be able to test everything without running a full deep learning model. But, these few steps will help you make sure everything's ready.

First, activate your conda environment,

Linux / Mac OS:

```
source activate deep-learning
```

Windows:

```
activate deep-learning
```

Run '**conda list**' and see the list of installed packages. You'll get a long list like the following,

```
conda list
# packages in environment at
C:\Users\UAMARTH\AppData\Local\Continuum\Ana
conda3\
envs\deep-learning:
#
asn1crypto              0.22.0
py35_0    conda-forge
backports.weakref       1.0rc1
<pip>
bkcharts                0.2
py35_0    conda-forge
bleach                  1.5.0
<pip>
bokeh                   0.12.6
py35_0    conda-forge
boost                   1.63.0
np112py35_vc14_6  [vc14]  conda-forge
boost-cpp               1.63.0
vc14_2   [vc14]  conda-forge
bzip2                   1.0.6
vc14_3   [vc14]
certifi                 2017.4.17
py35_0    conda-forge
cffi                    1.10.0
py35_0    conda-forge
chardet                 3.0.2
py35_1    conda-forge
```

```
click                              6.7
py35_0      conda-forge
...

...

...
```

Glance through the list to see if any package is missing.

Now, run the Python interpreter, and see whether it has the correct Python version (3.5.*) and architecture (64-Bit).

```
python
Python 3.5.3 |Continuum Analytics, Inc.|
(default, May 15 2017, 10:43:23) [MSC v.1900
64 bit (AMD64)] on win32
Type "help", "copyright", "credits" or
"license" for more information.
>>>
```

Import OpenCV. It should not give any errors.

```
>>> import cv2
>>>
```

Same for Dlib,

```
>>> import dlib
>>>
```

Import Keras. It will load the backend it's set to use.

```
>>> import keras
Using TensorFlow backend.
>>>
```

Finally, we're going to test TensorFlow. Run the following commands in the Python interpreter,

```
>>> import tensorflow as tf
>>> hello = tf.constant('Hello,
TensorFlow!')
>>> sess = tf.Session()
>>> print(sess.run(hello))
b'Hello, TensorFlow!'
>>> a = tf.constant(10)
>>> b = tf.constant(32)
>>> print(sess.run(a + b))
```

If you have the GPU version of TensorFlow installed, and have CUDA properly setup with its requirements, then you will see a TensorFlow device object being created as soon as you call tf.Session().

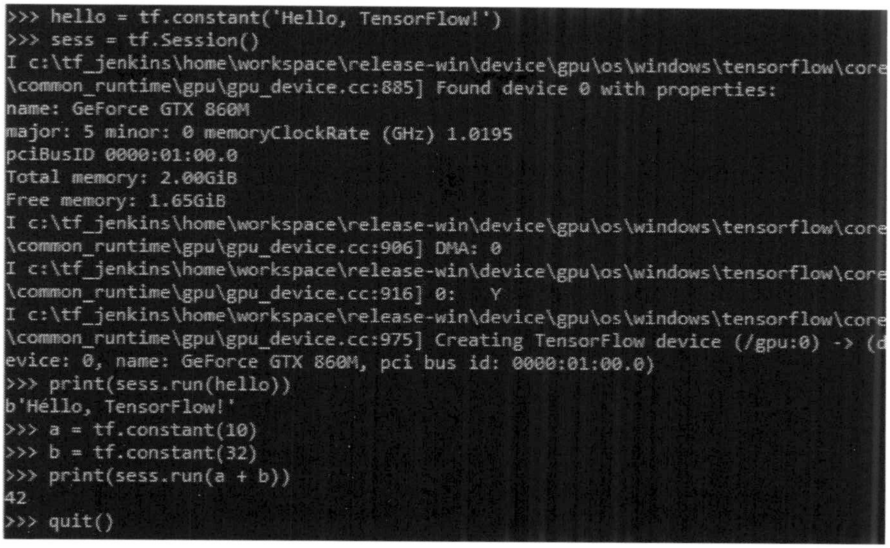

```
>>> hello = tf.constant('Hello, TensorFlow!')
>>> sess = tf.Session()
I c:\tf_jenkins\home\workspace\release-win\device\gpu\os\windows\tensorflow\core
\common_runtime\gpu\gpu_device.cc:885] Found device 0 with properties:
name: GeForce GTX 860M
major: 5 minor: 0 memoryClockRate (GHz) 1.0195
pciBusID 0000:01:00.0
Total memory: 2.00GiB
Free memory: 1.65GiB
I c:\tf_jenkins\home\workspace\release-win\device\gpu\os\windows\tensorflow\core
\common_runtime\gpu\gpu_device.cc:906] DMA: 0
I c:\tf_jenkins\home\workspace\release-win\device\gpu\os\windows\tensorflow\core
\common_runtime\gpu\gpu_device.cc:916] 0:    Y
I c:\tf_jenkins\home\workspace\release-win\device\gpu\os\windows\tensorflow\core
\common_runtime\gpu\gpu_device.cc:975] Creating TensorFlow device (/gpu:0) -> (d
evice: 0, name: GeForce GTX 860M, pci bus id: 0000:01:00.0)
>>> print(sess.run(hello))
b'Hello, TensorFlow!'
>>> a = tf.constant(10)
>>> b = tf.constant(32)
>>> print(sess.run(a + b))
42
>>> quit()
```

Figure 4-7: TensorFlow creating the device object on GPU

If all commands ran without errors, then we're good to go.

You can run "**quit()**" to exit the interpreter.

4.11 Summary

In this chapter, we learned how to setup all the tools needed to build Deep Learning models.

As a summary, here are all of the commands to install everything on a Linux machine in order (with the CPU version of TensorFlow),

```
conda create --name deep-learning python=3.5
numpy scipy scikit-learn scikit-image pillow
h5py matplotlib
```

```
source activate deep-learning

conda install -c conda-forge opencv=3.2.0

conda install -c conda-forge dlib=19.4

pip install --upgrade --no-deps
git+git://github.com/Theano/Theano.git

pip install keras

pip install --upgrade --no-deps
https://storage.googleapis.com/tensorflow/li
nux/cpu/tensorflow-1.2.1-cp35-cp35m-
linux_x86_64.whl

pip install
https://storage.googleapis.com/tensorflow/li
nux/cpu/tensorflow-1.2.1-cp35-cp35m-
linux_x86_64.whl
```

Now, you are ready to take on your first Deep Learning program.

Chapter 5 : Build Your First Deep Learning Model

We are now ready to start building our first Deep Learning model. But, where do we start?

In order to see deep learning in action, let's start with something that deep learning systems are extremely good at – a convolutional neural network built for image classification. For that, we'll build what's commonly considered the "Hello World" program of deep learning – that is to write a program to classify images of handwritten digits. Think of it as a simple OCR system.

But, don't we need a lot of data in order to train the system?

Well, lucky for us, since handwritten digits classification is a very popular problem to solve (even before deep learning), there is a publicly available dataset as such called the "**MNIST dataset**".

5.1   What is the MNIST Dataset?

Back in 1995, the National Institute of Standards and Technology (NIST) of US has created a dataset of handwritten characters to be used in machine learning and image processing systems. While this dataset worked for the most part, since the training and validation sets did not come from the same source, and due to some pre-processing applied on the images, there were some concerns about the validity of the dataset on a machine learning context.

So, in 1998, the data from the NIST dataset were cleaned up, normalized, and re-organized to resolve its issues, which created the MNIST dataset (**Modified National Institute of Standards and Technology dataset**). The MNIST contains 70,000 images – 60,000 training images, and 10,000 testing/validation images – of 28x28 pixels.

The MNIST dataset is publicly available from its official website (http://yann.lecun.com/exdb/mnist/). However, due to its popularity, many machine learning and deep learning frameworks either has it built-in, or provide utility methods to fetch and read the dataset. Keras, Scikit-Learn, and TensorFlow all provide such built-in methods, which spares us from having to retrieve, read, and format the data ourselves.

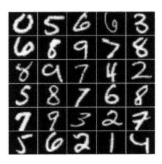

Figure 5-1: Few samples from the MNIST dataset

With a dataset at hand we now need to decide on the architecture of the convolutional neural network we're going to build. In deep learning, since there can be so many variations of the way we can structure a model, it's typically better to start with a known and proven deep learning model and then do adjustments on it. So, for our task, we'll choose the **LeNet** architecture.

5.2   The LeNet Model

LeNet is a 7-layer Convolutional Neural Network (CNN) introduced by Y. LeCun, L. Bottou, Y. Bengio, and P. Haffner. In their 1998 paper titled "Gradient-based learning applied to document recognition" they introduced LeNet-5, their 5th successful iteration of the architecture. It was designed specifically for handwritten and printed character recognition, so it fits perfectly with our requirements.

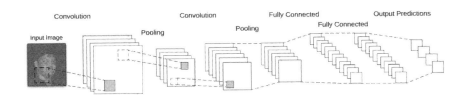

Figure 5-2: The LeNet Architecture

LeNet uses two sets of convolution operations. The first set uses 20 convolutional filters, and uses **ReLU** (Rectified Linear Units) as the non-linearity function, followed by a **Max-Pooling** layer. The second set uses

50 convolutional filters, again followed by ReLU and Max-Pooling. The output of these are then flattened, and sent through two Fully-connected (Dense) layers to get the output predictions.

The LeNet architecture is simple, but still gives excellent accuracy for small image classification tasks. And since it's small, it can be trained on a CPU as well.

5.3   Let's Code

We now have the data, and figured out the architecture for our deep learning model. Let's start coding.

We'll be using the TensorFlow backend with Keras, on Python 3.5.

Start a new Python file. We'll name it **lenet_mnist_keras.py**.

We start by importing the necessary packages,

```python
# import the necessary packages
from keras.datasets import mnist
from keras.optimizers import SGD
from keras.utils import np_utils


# imports used to build the deep learning
model
from keras.models import Sequential
from keras.layers.convolutional import
Conv2D
```

```
from keras.layers.convolutional import
MaxPooling2D
from keras.layers.core import Activation
from keras.layers.core import Flatten
from keras.layers.core import Dense


import numpy as np
import argparse
import cv2
import matplotlib.pyplot as plt
```

The **keras.datasets** package contains the built-in datasets of Keras. We import the MNIST dataset from it, while it contains several other datasets as well.

We import the **argparse** package to handle command line arguments.

OpenCV is used to display the results from evaluating the trained model.

It's always better to see how well a model gets trained. So, we import **Matplotlib** to graph the training history of our model.

There will be two phases to our digit classification system – training and evaluating. Training phase takes time, and is usually the most resource intensive phase. We certainly wouldn't want to run the training every time we run our program. So, we define a couple of command line arguments to trigger the two phases.

```
# Setup the argument parser to parse out
command line arguments
ap = argparse.ArgumentParser()
ap.add_argument("-t", "--train-model",
type=int, default=-1,
                help="(optional) Whether the
model should be trained on the MNIST
dataset. Defaults to no")
ap.add_argument("-s", "--save-trained",
type=int, default=-1,
                help="(optional) Whether the
trained models weights should be saved." +
                "Overwrites existing weights
file with the same name. Use with caution.
Defaults to no")
ap.add_argument("-w", "--weights", type=str,
default="data/lenet_weights.hdf5",
                help="(optional) Path to the
weights file. Defaults to
'data/lenet_weights.hdf5'")
args = vars(ap.parse_args())
```

We define three arguments.

- **--train-model** – indicates whether the model should be trained.
  Pass '1' to it to train the model.

- **--save-trained** – When the model is trained, we have the option to save the model weights to a file to be loaded back later. Pass '1' to this parameter to indicate to save the weights.

- **--weights** – By default, we will be saving the models weights to 'data/lenet_weights.hdf5' (Set by the 'default' parameter of this argument). If you want to override that path, you can pass a custom path to this parameter.

Now, we load and pre-process our dataset,

```python
# Get the MNIST dataset from Keras datasets
# If this is the first time you are fetching
the dataset, it will be downloaded
# File size will be ~10MB, and will placed
at ~/.keras/datasets/mnist.npz
print("[INFO] Loading the MNIST dataset...")
(trainData, trainLabels), (testData,
testLabels) = mnist.load_data()
# The data is already in the form of numpy
arrays,
# and already split to training and testing
datasets


# Reshape the data matrix from (samples,
height, width) to (samples, height, width,
depth)
# Depth (i.e. channels) is 1 since MNIST
only has grayscale images
```

```
trainData = trainData[:, :, :, np.newaxis]
testData = testData[:, :, :, np.newaxis]


# Rescale the data from values between [0 -
255] to [0 - 1.0]
trainData = trainData / 255.0
testData = testData / 255.0


# The labels comes as a single digit,
indicating the class.
# But we need a categorical vector as the
label. So we transform it.
# So that,
# '0' will become [1, 0, 0, 0, 0, 0, 0, 0,
0, 0]
# '1' will become [0, 1, 0, 0, 0, 0, 0, 0,
0, 0]
# '2' will become [0, 0, 1, 0, 0, 0, 0, 0,
0, 0]
# and so on...
trainLabels =
np_utils.to_categorical(trainLabels, 10)
testLabels =
np_utils.to_categorical(testLabels, 10)
```

Most of the 'cleaning up' of the dataset has been already done for us by
Keras. It's already in the format of numpy arrays, and already split to
training and testing data.

If this is the first time you are using the MNIST dataset from Keras, it will be downloaded (~10MB file size), and placed at **~/.keras/datasets/mnist.npz**.

The numpy arrays are in the format of **[samples, height, width]**. But Keras (and TensorFlow) expects one more dimension in the data arrays. Which is the '**depth**' – or the 'channels' – dimension. In a colour image, there would be three channels – Red, Green, and Blue. But since our digit images are grayscale images, there will only be one channel. So, we reshape the arrays to add one more axis, so that the arrays become **[samples, height, width, depth]** shaped.

Since these are image data – each value being the gay value of a pixel – the values are in the range of $0 - 255$. But for a neural network, it's better to always have the values in a range $0 - 1$. So, we divide the entire array by 255 to get it in range.

The labels for the dataset comes as single digits. But to train a neural network model, we need them as categorical vectors. We use the Keras numpy util function **to_categorical** to transform them so that,

'0' will become [1, 0, 0, 0, 0, 0, 0, 0, 0, 0]

'1' will become [0, 1, 0, 0, 0, 0, 0, 0, 0, 0]

'2' will become [0, 0, 1, 0, 0, 0, 0, 0, 0, 0]

And so on...

Now, we build our LeNet model,

```python
def build_lenet(width, height, depth,
classes, weightsPath=None):
    # Initialize the model
    model = Sequential()

    # The first set of CONV => RELU => POOL
layers
    model.add(Conv2D(20, (5, 5),
padding="same",
                        input_shape=(height,
width, depth)))
    model.add(Activation("relu"))
    model.add(MaxPooling2D(pool_size=(2, 2),
strides=(2, 2)))

    # The second set of CONV => RELU => POOL
layers
    model.add(Conv2D(50, (5, 5),
padding="same"))
    model.add(Activation("relu"))
    model.add(MaxPooling2D(pool_size=(2, 2),
strides=(2, 2)))

    # The set of FC => RELU layers
    model.add(Flatten())
    model.add(Dense(500))
```

```
    model.add(Activation("relu"))


    # The softmax classifier
    model.add(Dense(classes))
    model.add(Activation("softmax"))


    # If a weights path is supplied, then
load the weights
    if weightsPath is not None:
        model.load_weights(weightsPath)


    # Return the constructed network
architecture
    return model
```

We define a function – build_lenet – which takes five parameters: the width, height, and depth of the input, the number of classes, and the path to the model weights file if given.

We use the Keras Sequential model to build our network. The Keras Sequential model makes building sequential network architectures (where all the layers are stacked up sequentially) much simpler. For more complex, non-sequential architectures (such as Inception modules) Keras provides the functional API. But for simple sequential ones like LeNet, the Sequential model is the easiest.

We start with the first Convolutional, ReLU, and Pooling layer set. In the sequential model, the first layer needs to know the shape of the input to expect, so we pass it with the **input_shape** parameter. The subsequent layers can infer the shape on their own. We first define 20 convolutional filters of size 5x5, followed by a ReLU activation, and a Max-Pooling layer of 2x2.

The second set of Convolutional, ReLU, and Pooling layers are almost the same, with the number of convolutional filters increased to 50.

We then flatten the input, and add a **Dense** (fully-connected) layer of 500 units.

The final layer is again a Dense layer, where the number of units is equal to the number of output classes of our data. We set a **Softmax** classifier as the activation of it.

If a path to a model weights file is passed, we load the weights to the constructed model. Otherwise, we return just the model.

Once the model is constructed (and optionally, the weights loaded) we specify an optimizer for it and compile it,

```
# Build and Compile the model
print("[INFO] Building and compiling the
LeNet model...")
opt = SGD(lr=0.01)
model = build_lenet(width=28, height=28,
depth=1, classes=10,

weightsPath=args["weights"] if
args["train_model"] <= 0 else None)
```

```
model.compile(loss="categorical_crossentropy
",
                    optimizer=opt,
metrics=["accuracy"])
```

Here, we are using the SGD Optimizer (**Stochastic Gradient Descent**), with a learning rate of 0.01 (set by the **lr** parameter).

Now, we are ready to train our model,

```
# Check the argument whether to train the
model
if args["train_model"] > 0:
    print("[INFO] Training the model...")

    history = model.fit(trainData,
trainLabels,
                        batch_size=128,
                        epochs=20,

validation_data=(testData, testLabels),
                        verbose=1)

    # Use the test data to evaluate the
model
    print("[INFO] Evaluating the model...")
```

```
    (loss, accuracy) = model.evaluate(
        testData, testLabels,
    batch_size=128, verbose=1)


    print("[INFO] accuracy:
    {:.2f}%".format(accuracy * 100))
```

We pass our trainData and trainLabels – which we pre-processed earlier – in to the **model.fit()** function.

Deep learning models are rarely trained single sample at a time. Here also, we are training in batches. We set the batch size to 128.

We set the number of epochs to train to 20.

We also pass in the test data to the validation_data parameter, which is used to track the accuracy and loss across training batches.

Once the training is complete, we use the **model.evaluate()** function to evaluate the model with the entire test dataset.

You will notice that the model.fit() returns an object called '**history**'. It contains the accuracy and loss matrices of the model as it trained. We can use this history object to graph the training history matrices. We define a new function – graph_training_history – to accept the history object,

```
def graph_training_history(history):
    plt.figure(1)


    # summarize history for accuracy
```

```
    plt.subplot(211)
    plt.plot(history.history['acc'])
    plt.plot(history.history['val_acc'])
    plt.title('model accuracy')
    plt.ylabel('accuracy')
    plt.xlabel('epoch')
    plt.legend(['train', 'test'], loc='upper
left')

    # summarize history for loss

    plt.subplot(212)
    plt.plot(history.history['loss'])
    plt.plot(history.history['val_loss'])
    plt.title('model loss')
    plt.ylabel('loss')
    plt.xlabel('epoch')
    plt.legend(['train', 'test'], loc='upper
left')

    plt.show()
```

We pass the history object to this function after the model training completes,

```
    # Visualize the training history
    graph_training_history(history)
```

The history object contains four keys: **['acc', 'loss', 'val_acc', 'val_loss']**.

We use Matplotlib to draw the graph. We define two subplots to draw the accuracy matrices and the loss matrices for training and validation separately.

Once all the training and validation is complete, we save the model weights to a file,

```
# Check the argument on whether to save the
model weights to file
if args["save_trained"] > 0:
    print("[INFO] Saving the model weights
to file...")
    model.save_weights(args["weights"],
overwrite=True)
```

We use the value of the "weights" command line argument as the path, which is by default set to "data/lenet_weights.hdf5" if you didn't override it.

Now the model is ready. Let's test it out on a couple of digits,

```
# Randomly select a few samples from the
test dataset to evaluate
```

```python
for i in np.random.choice(np.arange(0,
len(testLabels)), size=(10,)):
    # Use the model to classify the digit
    probs =
model.predict(testData[np.newaxis, i])
    prediction = probs.argmax(axis=1)


    # Convert the digit data to a color
image
    image = (testData[i] *
255).astype("uint8")
    image = cv2.cvtColor(image,
cv2.COLOR_GRAY2RGB)


    # The images are in 28x28 size. Much too
small to see properly
    # So, we resize them to 280x280 for
viewing
    image = cv2.resize(image, (280, 280),
interpolation=cv2.INTER_LINEAR)


    # Add the predicted value on to the
image
    cv2.putText(image, str(prediction[0]),
 (20, 40),
              cv2.FONT_HERSHEY_DUPLEX,
1.5, (0, 255, 0), 1)
```

```
    # Show the image and prediction
    print("[INFO] Predicted: {}, Actual:
{}".format(
        prediction[0],
np.argmax(testLabels[i])))
    cv2.imshow("Digit", image)
    cv2.waitKey(0)


cv2.destroyAllWindows()
```

We pick 10 random digits from the test dataset.

We then pass each of these images to our models' predict function to get a prediction of what that digit is. The predict function — much like the train function — expects a batch of input for predicting. Since we're only passing one sample at a time, we add a new axis to the data array — testData[np.newaxis, i] — to indicate that there's only one sample in this input.

The predictions comes as a vector, so we take the **argmax** of it to get the label of the prediction.

We now have the prediction. But rather than printing it out in the console alone, we want to display it along with the digit. We're going to use OpenCV for that. But, we need to do some slight adjustments to the data before we're able to show them on OpenCV.

Remember that earlier, we rescaled all the data to be in the range of [0 − 1.0]? Now, we need to rescale it back to [0 − 255]. So, we multiply everything by 255.

OpenCV expects the image data to be unsigned 8-bit integers. So, we convert the entire array to 'uint8' format with **astype("uint8")**.

Now the image is in grayscale format. We convert it to a colour image by calling **cv2.cvtColor(image, cv2.COLOR_GRAY2RGB)**. The image will still look grayscale. But now, we can draw text on it with colour.

And finally, having the images at 28x28 pixels size is much too small. So, we resize them to 280x280 size using **cv2.resize()** function.

With the image data ready, we put the predicted digit value on the top left corner of the image and display it. By specifying **cv2.waitKey(0)** we keep the window open till any key is pressed. And since we are in a loop we can switch through the 10 random digits we choose from the test dataset.

We also print the prediction, and the actual value to the console.

That completes the coding of our first Deep Learning model. The complete code can be found in the Appendix II of this book.

5.4   Running our first Deep Learning model

We're now ready to run our model. A couple of pre-checks to do,

1. Check whether you have all the required libraries installed: Keras, TensorFlow, OpenCV, Matplotlib.
2. Have you activated your conda environment?

3. Create a directory named 'data' where your lenet_mnist_keras.py file is located. This is where the model weights will be saved by default. Make sure the directory is writable.

Once all pre-checks are done, we run our code.

Since this is the first run, we need to train the model. So, we set the command line arguments to train the model, and save the weights of the trained model,

```
python lenet_mnist_keras.py --train-model 1 --
save-trained 1
```

Keras will automatically download the MNIST dataset if this is the first time it's being used. The download is about 10MB so shouldn't' take long.

Once the data is downloaded, the model built, and compiled, it will start the training.

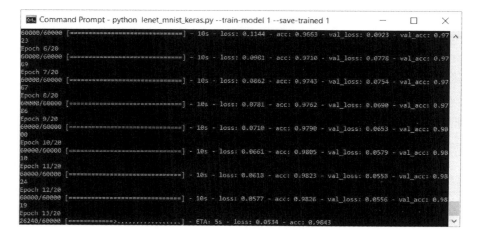

Figure 5-3: Model being trained

The training will run for 20 epochs.

If you're running this on GPU, the training will take less than 2 minutes. On a CPU however, it may take up to 30 minutes.

The console will show the progress of the training, accuracy and loss of training and validation.

Once the training is complete, it'll evaluate the model on the test dataset and give the final accuracy value.

```
60000/60000 [==============================] - 10s - loss: 0.0391 - acc: 0.9884
- val_loss: 0.0428 - val_acc: 0.9851
[INFO] Evaluating the model...
9984/10000 [==========================>.] - ETA: 0s[INFO] accuracy: 98.51%
```

Figure 5-4: Final evaluation of the model

We'll be getting about 98% – 99% accuracy, which is actually pretty good, even for a Deep Learning model.

Once the evaluation step is done, Matplotlib will open a window to show the training history of the model.

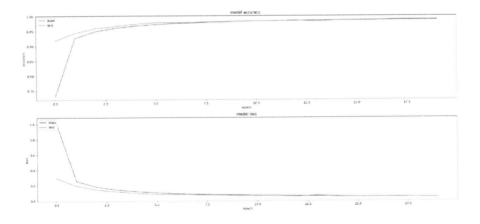

Figure 5-5: The model training history

The accuracy and the loss matrices of the training graph looks good. It doesn't look like it's overfitting to the training data, which is good.

The code execution will be on hold until you close the Matplotlib window. So, remember to close it once you reviewed the graph.

Now, the fun part. OpenCV will open the 10 random test digits one at a time, along with the predicted value of the digit (in green at the top-left of the image). Here are some examples,

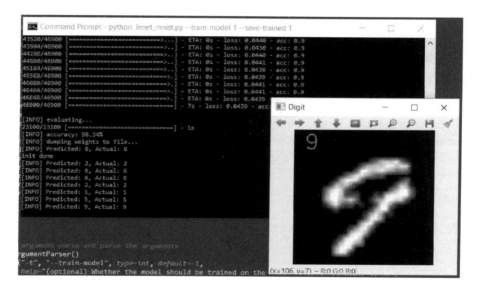

Figure 5-6: Model prediction - Digit '9'

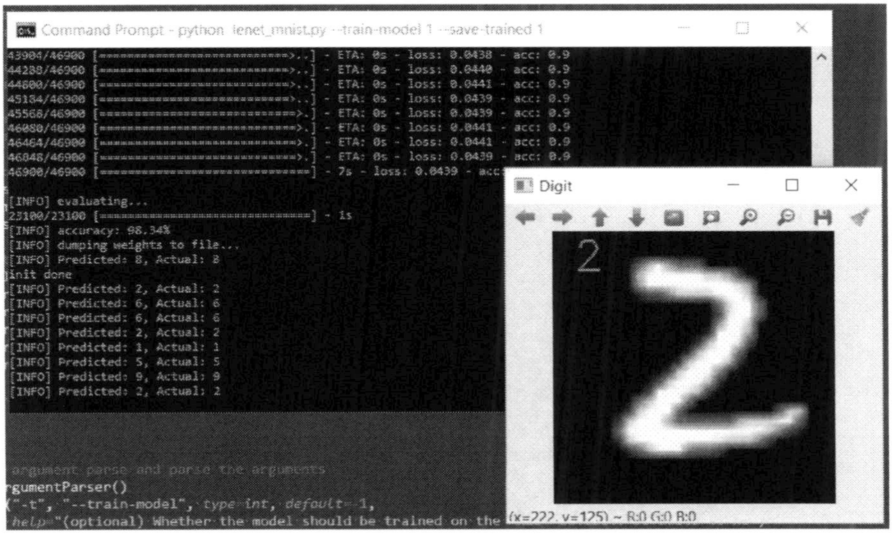

Figure 5-7: Model prediction - Digit '2'

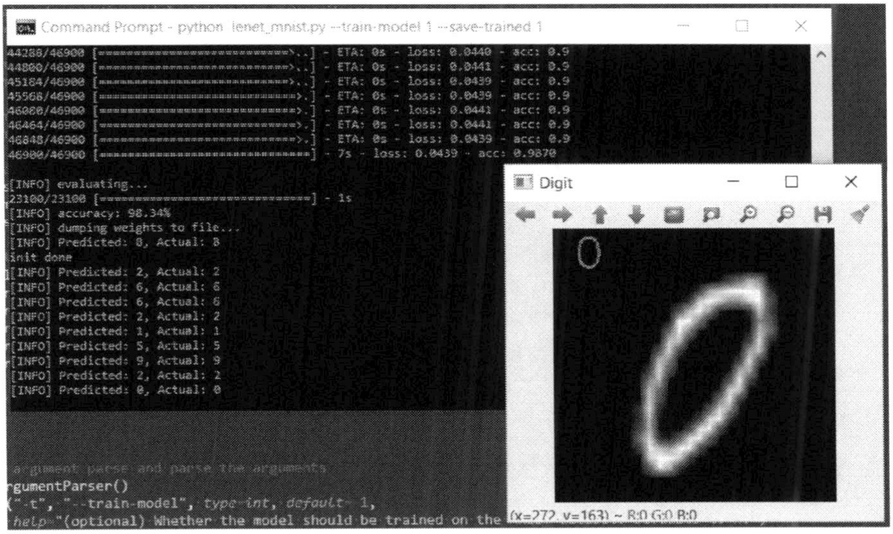

Figure 5-8: Model prediction - Digit '0'

You can switch through the digits by pressing any key.

Note: In some versions of OpenCV, there's a bug in the code for opening an image window. If you try to manually close the window, the code execution might get stuck. So, better to just let the code close it properly with **cv2.destroyAllWindows()**.

Along with showing the digit, we also print the predicted and the actual values to the console,

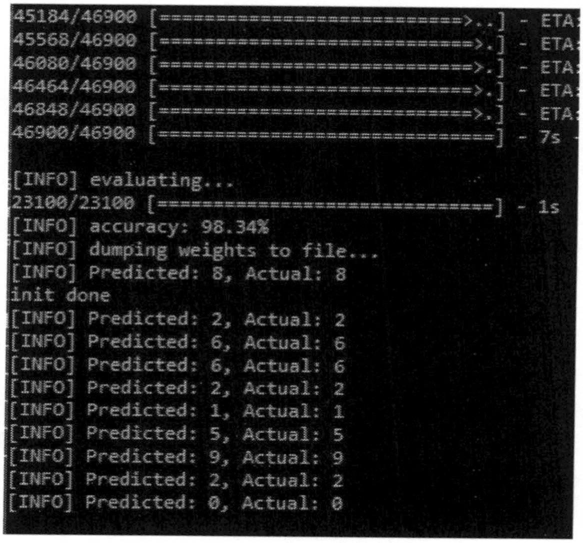

Figure 5-9: The testing digit predictions and actual values printed on the console

After training our model, the model weights will be saved to **data/lenet_weights.hdf5**. So, you can run the model again without training using,

```
python lenet_mnist_keras.py
```

Once you're satisfied with how the LeNet model classifies digits, you can try tweaking the model and see how it affects results. Here are few things you can try out,

- Change the number of convolutional filters, and see how it affects the training (via the training history graph)
- Add more convolutional layers, and see whether it improves the model. See how it affects the training time as well. And see how many layers you can add before the model starts to become worse.
- Add more dense layers. Is the model starting to overfit?

You can detect when the model is overfitting by looking at the loss metrics. If the validation loss stops dropping while the training loss continues to drop as the training progresses, then the model is overfitting. Which means the model has basically 'memorized' our training samples, but has not learn to generalize the problem, causing it to fail on the unseen samples (here, the validation samples).

Chapter 6 : What Can We Do Next?

We have now setup the tools needed to build our Deep Learning models, and we have built, tested, and fiddled with our first Deep Learning model. We now have a little taste of what a Deep Learning model looks like.

What can we do next?

6.1 Try out built-in Keras Applications

We learned about the milestones of deep learning on Chapter 2. Would you like to try some of them hands on? Keras has made it easy for us, since Keras has the most popular deep learning models built-in. The *keras.applications* package contains the following models,

- VGG16
- VGG19
- ResNet50
- InceptionV3
- Xception (Only with TensorFlow)

- MobileNet (Only with TensorFlow)

Out of these, VGG16, VGG19, ResNet50, and InceptionV3 models works with both TensorFlow and Theano backends. The Xception model only works with TensorFlow, since it relies on *SeparableConvolution* layers. Likewise, the MobileNet model also only works with TensorFlow, since it relies on *DepthwiseConvolution* layers.

Keras not only provides the models, it also provides the model weights for each of the models trained in the ImageNet dataset. The weights aren't built into Keras, but rather – because of the large size of the weight files – gets downloaded the first time the weights are used for a particular model. You just need to specify **weights='imagenet'**, and Keras will take care of downloading the correct weights file based on the backend you're using. The downloaded weights files will be placed under **~/.keras/models/** (or **%USERPROFILE%\.keras\models** on Windows).

If you want – rather than using the provided ImageNet weights – you can of course load any compatible weights file of your own, by using the **model. load_weights()** function by passing the path to the weights file. Or, you can simply get the bare model (without weights loaded) and train it on your own dataset.

You can also load only the convolutional portion of a model (without the final dense layers). This is particularly useful for extracting bottleneck features from a pre-trained model for Transfer Learning (which we'll talk about in a bit). You just need to specify **include_top=False**. If you're loading the ImageNet weights (by specifying weights='imagenet'), Keras will take care of loading only the weights for the convolutional layers, as they already have separate weights files for models with and without the top layers.

Keras also provides two other useful functions per model for working with ImageNet data: **preprocess_input** and **decode_predictions**.

The preprocess_input function runs the input data through the same pre-processing steps done in the original ImageNet dataset which the model was trained on. The decode_predictions will let you filter the top n number of predictions with highest confidence (out of 1000 classes of ImageNet), and get the text label for the prediction classes.

Here's an example code to predict an image through the VGG16 model,

```python
from keras.applications.vgg16 import VGG16
from keras.preprocessing import image
from keras.applications.vgg16 import
preprocess_input, decode_predictions
import numpy as np


model = VGG16(weights='imagenet')


img_path = 'Data/Jellyfish.jpg'
img = image.load_img(img_path,
target_size=(224, 224))
img_data = image.img_to_array(img)
img_data = np.expand_dims(img_data, axis=0)
img_data = preprocess_input(img_data)


preds = model.predict(img_data)
```

```
# decode the results into a list of tuples
(class, description, probability)
print('Predicted:',
decode_predictions(preds, top=3)[0])
```

The code would give an output like this,

```
Predicted: [('n01910747', 'jellyfish',
0.99959451), ('n02219486', 'ant',
0.0001532107), ('n01930112', 'nematode',
5.4959004e-05)]
```

More examples can be found in the Appendix II.

6.2   Get into the code of Deep Learning models

Keras applications are great when you want to try out well known deep learning models. But we don't really see the internal code of them. Nor, can we try and tweak their structures to see how it affects the model.

Lucky for us, the people who make Keras has a Git repository with all the deep learning models.

The repository is named "**Deep Learning Models**", and you can find it here: https://github.com/fchollet/deep-learning-models

The repository contains the code for the same models as those which are built-into Keras,

- VGG16 - https://github.com/fchollet/deep-learning-models/blob/master/vgg16.py

- VGG19 - https://github.com/fchollet/deep-learning-models/blob/master/vgg19.py

- ResNet50 - https://github.com/fchollet/deep-learning-models/blob/master/resnet50.py

- InceptionV3 - https://github.com/fchollet/deep-learning-models/blob/master/inception_v3.py

- Xception - https://github.com/fchollet/deep-learning-models/blob/master/xception.py

- MobileNet - https://github.com/fchollet/deep-learning-models/blob/master/mobilenet.py

You can also manually download the weights files for each model from the releases page of the repository: https://github.com/fchollet/deep-learning-models/releases

The code uses the Keras Functional API, rather than the Sequential model. This is because some non-sequential models – such as InceptionV3 – can only be built using the functional API. Although models such as VGG can be built with the Keras Sequential model, they have kept the code consistent by using the functional API for all.

The code for VGG16 looks like this,

(Code extracted from https://github.com/fchollet/deep-learning-models/blob/master/vgg16.py)

```
# Block 1
x = Conv2D(64, (3, 3), activation='relu',
padding='same',
name='block1_conv1')(img_input)
x = Conv2D(64, (3, 3), activation='relu',
padding='same', name='block1_conv2')(x)
x = MaxPooling2D((2, 2), strides=(2, 2),
name='block1_pool')(x)

# Block 2
x = Conv2D(128, (3, 3), activation='relu',
padding='same', name='block2_conv1')(x)
x = Conv2D(128, (3, 3), activation='relu',
padding='same', name='block2_conv2')(x)
x = MaxPooling2D((2, 2), strides=(2, 2),
name='block2_pool')(x)

# Block 3
x = Conv2D(256, (3, 3), activation='relu',
padding='same', name='block3_conv1')(x)
x = Conv2D(256, (3, 3), activation='relu',
padding='same', name='block3_conv2')(x)
x = Conv2D(256, (3, 3), activation='relu',
padding='same', name='block3_conv3')(x)
```

```python
x = MaxPooling2D((2, 2), strides=(2, 2),
name='block3_pool')(x)


# Block 4
x = Conv2D(512, (3, 3), activation='relu',
padding='same', name='block4_conv1')(x)
x = Conv2D(512, (3, 3), activation='relu',
padding='same', name='block4_conv2')(x)
x = Conv2D(512, (3, 3), activation='relu',
padding='same', name='block4_conv3')(x)
x = MaxPooling2D((2, 2), strides=(2, 2),
name='block4_pool')(x)


# Block 5
x = Conv2D(512, (3, 3), activation='relu',
padding='same', name='block5_conv1')(x)
x = Conv2D(512, (3, 3), activation='relu',
padding='same', name='block5_conv2')(x)
x = Conv2D(512, (3, 3), activation='relu',
padding='same', name='block5_conv3')(x)
x = MaxPooling2D((2, 2), strides=(2, 2),
name='block5_pool')(x)


if include_top:
    # Classification block
    x = Flatten(name='flatten')(x)
    x = Dense(4096, activation='relu',
name='fc1')(x)
```

```
    x = Dense(4096, activation='relu',
name='fc2')(x)
    x = Dense(classes,
activation='softmax', name='predictions')(x)


. . . . . . . .
. . . . . . .
. . . . . . .


model = Model(inputs, x, name='vgg16')
```

If you want to build the VGG16 model with the Sequential model, then you would be able to achieve it with the following code,

```
input_shape=(224,224,3)

model = Sequential()
model.add(ZeroPadding2D((1,1),input_shape=in
put_shape))
model.add(Conv2D(64, (3, 3),
activation='relu'))
model.add(ZeroPadding2D((1,1)))
model.add(Conv2D(64, (3, 3),
activation='relu'))
model.add(MaxPooling2D((2,2),
strides=(2,2)))

model.add(ZeroPadding2D((1,1)))
```

```python
model.add(Conv2D(128, (3, 3),
activation='relu'))
model.add(ZeroPadding2D((1,1)))
model.add(Conv2D(128, (3, 3),
activation='relu'))
model.add(MaxPooling2D((2,2),
strides=(2,2)))

model.add(ZeroPadding2D((1,1)))
model.add(Conv2D(256, (3, 3),
activation='relu'))
model.add(ZeroPadding2D((1,1)))
model.add(Conv2D(256, (3, 3),
activation='relu'))
model.add(ZeroPadding2D((1,1)))
model.add(Conv2D(256, (3, 3),
activation='relu'))
model.add(MaxPooling2D((2,2),
strides=(2,2)))

model.add(ZeroPadding2D((1,1)))
model.add(Conv2D(512, (3, 3),
activation='relu'))
model.add(ZeroPadding2D((1,1)))
model.add(Conv2D(512, (3, 3),
activation='relu'))
model.add(ZeroPadding2D((1,1)))
```

```
model.add(Conv2D(512, (3, 3),
activation='relu'))
model.add(MaxPooling2D((2,2),
strides=(2,2)))

model.add(ZeroPadding2D((1,1)))
model.add(Conv2D(512, (3, 3),
activation='relu'))
model.add(ZeroPadding2D((1,1)))
model.add(Conv2D(512, (3, 3),
activation='relu'))
model.add(ZeroPadding2D((1,1)))
model.add(Conv2D(512, (3, 3),
activation='relu'))
model.add(MaxPooling2D((2,2),
strides=(2,2)))

model.add(Flatten())
model.add(Dense(4096, activation='relu'))
model.add(Dropout(0.5))
model.add(Dense(4096, activation='relu'))
model.add(Dropout(0.5))
model.add(Dense(1000, activation='softmax'))
```

Try and go through the two blocks of code – the functional and the
sequential – and see whether you can see the pattern on how they map
to each other.

Note: One thing you might notice is that the code for the sequential model uses **ZeroPadding2D** layers. These can actually be removed by setting **padding='same'** in the Conv2D (and keeping **strides=(1, 1)**, which is the default), as Keras will automatically apply the padding in that case.

So, what can we do with knowing the code of deep learning models? The same thing we did with LeNet. Since these are 'proven' models for certain tasks (such as image classification), you can try using these models for the problems you're trying to solve, and see how they perform. You can then try to tweak them to fit for the exact problem you're solving.

6.3   Try Transfer Learning

We saw how exceptionally well deep learning models trained on the ImageNet dataset perform. With 1000 categories for classification, those models are able to achieve over 95% accuracy. So, you might be thinking, why not train our own classification model, for our own classification categories?

But, you might find that building a classifications system from scratch – even with deep learning – is not an easy task. In order to get a sufficient accuracy from your model, without it overfitting, would require a lot of training data. The ImageNet has millions of data samples. Which is why the models trained on them perform so well. But for us to find or build a training dataset of that level for the classification task we plan on building would be practically infeasible.

So, should we give up trying to build our own classification model?

Not really. Because, deep learning again has the solution.

Deep learning supports an immensely useful feature called 'Transfer Learning'. Basically, you are able to take a pre-trained deep learning model – which is trained on a large-scale dataset such as ImageNet – and re-purpose it to handle an entirely different problem. The idea is that since the model has already learned certain features from a large dataset (think back to Hierarchical Feature Learning), it may be able to use those features as a base to learn the particular classification problem we present it with.

The basic technique to get transfer learning working is to get a pre-trained model (with the weights loaded) and remove the final fully-connected layers from that model. We then use the remaining portion of the model as a feature extractor for our smaller dataset. These extracted features are called "**Bottleneck Features**", which are the last activation maps before the fully-connected layers in the original model. We then train a small fully-connected network on those extracted bottleneck features in order to get the classes we need as outputs for our problem.

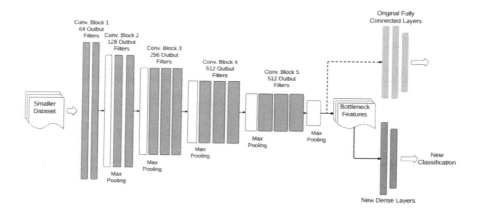

Figure 6-1: How bottleneck feature extraction works

With Keras, having the models built-in, with their pre-trained weights, and having an option to remove the fully connected layers just by specifying include_top=False couldn't make our task easier.

As we discussed earlier, setting **include_top=False** when creating a model from Keras applications will create the model without the final block of dense layers.

```
model =
applications.VGG16(include_top=False,
weights='imagenet')
```

Keras also has set of utility methods – the **ImageDataGenerator** and the related generator functions for training and validation – that would help us batch process image data, which simplifies loading and pre-processing images. These comes handy when building a transfer learning model.

If you would like to attempt to implement a transfer learning model there's a complete code example in the Appendix II. For a more detailed guide, you can check out the **Using Bottleneck Features for Multi-Class Classification in Keras and TensorFlow** article at **Codes of Interest** (http://www.codesofinterest.com/2017/08/bottleneck-features-multi-class-classification-keras.html).

The ImageDataGenerator methods has few more tricks we can use. Through them, you can introduce augmentations – random transformations and normalization – to your data which, if done correctly, will further reduce the chance of overfitting. Check out the **Image Preprocessing** section (https://keras.io/preprocessing/image/) in the Keras documentation and give it a try also.

Ready for more? Head over to **Codes of Interest** (www.codesofinterest.com), your one-stop source for hands-on Deep Learning and Computer Vision.

References and Useful Links

Installation Guides at Codes of Interest -
http://www.codesofinterest.com/search/label/Installation

Troubleshooting Guides at Codes of Interest -
http://www.codesofinterest.com/search/label/Troubleshooting

Deep Learning and Computer Vision Tutorials at Codes of Interest -
http://www.codesofinterest.com/search/label/Tutorial

More Resources - http://www.codesofinterest.com/p/resources.html

Anaconda Python Homepage - https://www.continuum.io/

OpenCV Homepage - http://opencv.org/

Dlib Homepage - http://dlib.net/

Theano Homepage - http://www.deeplearning.net/software/theano/

Keras Homepage - https://keras.io/

TensorFlow Homepage - https://www.tensorflow.org/

OpenBLAS Homepage - http://www.openblas.net/

NVIDIA CUDA Homepage -
http://www.nvidia.com/object/cuda_home_new.html

cuDNN Homepage - https://developer.nvidia.com/cudnn

The Original NIST Database -
https://www.nist.gov/sites/default/files/documents/srd/nistsd19.pdf

The MNIST Database - http://yann.lecun.com/exdb/mnist/

The LeNet Model - http://yann.lecun.com/exdb/lenet/

Keras Functional API - https://keras.io/getting-started/functional-api-guide/

Keras Sequential Model - https://keras.io/getting-started/sequential-model-guide/

Keras Applications - https://keras.io/applications/

The 1000 Layer ResNet Model -
https://github.com/KaimingHe/resnet-1k-layers

Keras Image Pre-processing options -
https://keras.io/preprocessing/image/

Switching between TensorFlow and Theano on Keras -
http://www.codesofinterest.com/2016/11/switching-between-tensorflow-and-theano.html

What is the image_dim_ordering parameter in Keras, and why is it important - http://www.codesofinterest.com/2016/11/keras-image-dim-ordering.html

image_data_format vs. image_dim_ordering in Keras v2 -
http://www.codesofinterest.com/2017/05/image-data-format-vs-image-dim-ordering-keras-v2.html

Getting Theano working with OpenBLAS on Windows -
http://www.codesofinterest.com/2016/10/getting-theano-working-with-openblas-on.html

Appendix I – Diagrams

Note: These diagrams can be viewed at

http://www.codesofinterest.com/p/build-deeper.html

VGG Net

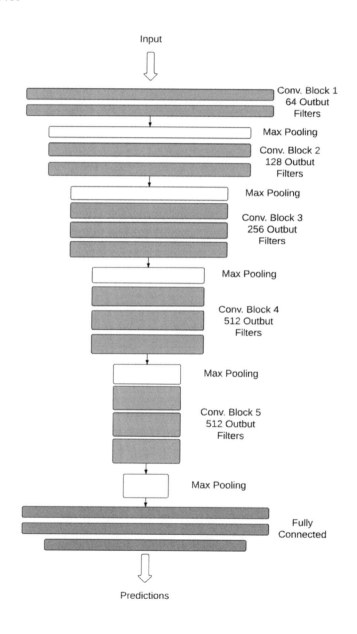

GoogLeNet

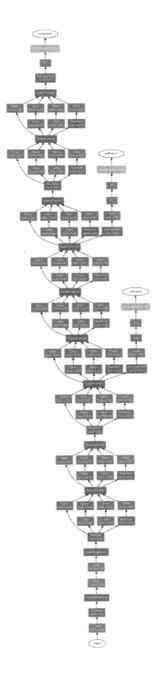

Image source: Research Paper - Going Deeper with Convolutions

Microsoft ResNet

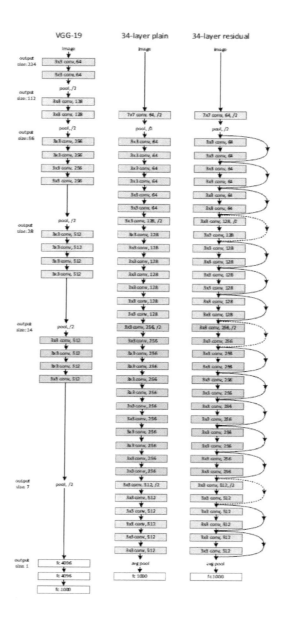

Image source: Research Paper - Deep Residual Learning for Image Recognition

Appendix II – Code

Note: These code samples are available at

http://www.codesofinterest.com/p/build-deeper.html

The complete code for our LeNet Model for the MNIST Dataset.

```
# How to use
#
# Train the model and save the model weights
# python lenet_mnist_keras.py --train-model
1 --save-trained 1
#
# Train the model and save the model wights
to a give directory
# python lenet_mnist_keras.py --train-model
1 --save-trained 1 --weights
data/lenet_weights.hdf5
#
# Evaluate the model from pre-trained model
wights
# python lenet_mnist_keras.py
#
# Evaluate the model from pre-trained model
wights from a give directory
# python lenet_mnist_keras.py --weights
data/lenet_weights.hdf5
```

```python
# import the necessary packages
from keras.datasets import mnist
from keras.optimizers import SGD
from keras.utils import np_utils

# imports used to build the deep learning
model
from keras.models import Sequential
from keras.layers.convolutional import
Conv2D
from keras.layers.convolutional import
MaxPooling2D
from keras.layers.core import Activation
from keras.layers.core import Flatten
from keras.layers.core import Dense

import numpy as np
import argparse
import cv2
import matplotlib.pyplot as plt

# Setup the argument parser to parse out
command line arguments
ap = argparse.ArgumentParser()
ap.add_argument("-t", "--train-model",
type=int, default=-1,
```

```python
                    help="(optional) Whether the
model should be trained on the MNIST
dataset. Defaults to no")
ap.add_argument("-s", "--save-trained",
type=int, default=-1,
                  help="(optional) Whether the
trained models weights should be saved." +
                  "Overwrites existing weights
file with the same name. Use with caution.
Defaults to no")
ap.add_argument("-w", "--weights", type=str,
default="data/lenet_weights.hdf5",
                  help="(optional) Path to the
weights file. Defaults to
'data/lenet_weights.hdf5'")
args = vars(ap.parse_args())


def build_lenet(width, height, depth,
classes, weightsPath=None):
    # Initialize the model
    model = Sequential()

    # The first set of CONV => RELU => POOL
layers
    model.add(Conv2D(20, (5, 5),
padding="same",
```

```python
                input_shape=(height,
width, depth)))
    model.add(Activation("relu"))
    model.add(MaxPooling2D(pool_size=(2, 2),
strides=(2, 2)))


    # The second set of CONV => RELU => POOL
layers
    model.add(Conv2D(50, (5, 5),
padding="same"))
    model.add(Activation("relu"))
    model.add(MaxPooling2D(pool_size=(2, 2),
strides=(2, 2)))


    # The set of FC => RELU layers
    model.add(Flatten())
    model.add(Dense(500))
    model.add(Activation("relu"))


    # The softmax classifier
    model.add(Dense(classes))
    model.add(Activation("softmax"))


    # If a weights path is supplied, then
load the weights
    if weightsPath is not None:
        model.load_weights(weightsPath)
```

```python
    # Return the constructed network
architecture
    return model


def graph_training_history(history):
    plt.figure(1)

    # summarize history for accuracy

    plt.subplot(211)
    plt.plot(history.history['acc'])
    plt.plot(history.history['val_acc'])
    plt.title('model accuracy')
    plt.ylabel('accuracy')
    plt.xlabel('epoch')
    plt.legend(['train', 'test'], loc='upper
left')

    # summarize history for loss

    plt.subplot(212)
    plt.plot(history.history['loss'])
    plt.plot(history.history['val_loss'])
    plt.title('model loss')
    plt.ylabel('loss')
    plt.xlabel('epoch')
```

```python
    plt.legend(['train', 'test'], loc='upper
left')


    plt.show()



# Get the MNIST dataset from Keras datasets
# If this is the first time you are fetching
the dataset, it will be downloaded
# File size will be ~10MB, and will placed
at ~/.keras/datasets/mnist.npz
print("[INFO] Loading the MNIST dataset...")
(trainData, trainLabels), (testData,
testLabels) = mnist.load_data()
# The data is already in the form of numpy
arrays,
# and already split to training and testing
datasets


# Reshape the data matrix from (samples,
height, width) to (samples, height, width,
depth)
# Depth (i.e. channels) is 1 since MNIST
only has grayscale images
trainData = trainData[:, :, :, np.newaxis]
testData = testData[:, :, :, np.newaxis]
```

```python
# Rescale the data from values between [0 -
255] to [0 - 1.0]
trainData = trainData / 255.0
testData = testData / 255.0


# The labels comes as a single digit,
indicating the class.
# But we need a categorical vector as the
label. So we transform it.
# So that,
# '0' will become [1, 0, 0, 0, 0, 0, 0, 0,
0, 0]
# '1' will become [0, 1, 0, 0, 0, 0, 0, 0,
0, 0]
# '2' will become [0, 0, 1, 0, 0, 0, 0, 0,
0, 0]
# and so on...
trainLabels =
np_utils.to_categorical(trainLabels, 10)
testLabels =
np_utils.to_categorical(testLabels, 10)


# Build and Compile the model
print("[INFO] Building and compiling the
LeNet model...")
opt = SGD(lr=0.01)
model = build_lenet(width=28, height=28,
depth=1, classes=10,
```

```python
	weightsPath=args["weights"] if
	args["train_model"] <= 0 else None)
	model.compile(loss="categorical_crossentropy
	",
	                optimizer=opt,
	metrics=["accuracy"])


	# Check the argument whether to train the
	model
	if args["train_model"] > 0:
	    print("[INFO] Training the model...")


	    history = model.fit(trainData,
	trainLabels,
	                        batch_size=128,
	                        epochs=20,

	validation_data=(testData, testLabels),
	                        verbose=1)


	    # Use the test data to evaluate the
	model
	    print("[INFO] Evaluating the model...")


	    (loss, accuracy) = model.evaluate(
	        testData, testLabels,
	batch_size=128, verbose=1)
```

```python
    print("[INFO] accuracy:
{:.2f}%".format(accuracy * 100))


    # Visualize the training history
    graph_training_history(history)


# Check the argument on whether to save the
model weights to file
if args["save_trained"] > 0:
    print("[INFO] Saving the model weights
to file...")
    model.save_weights(args["weights"],
overwrite=True)


# Training of the model is now complete


# Randomly select a few samples from the
test dataset to evaluate
for i in np.random.choice(np.arange(0,
len(testLabels)), size=(10,)):
    # Use the model to classify the digit
    probs =
model.predict(testData[np.newaxis, i])
    prediction = probs.argmax(axis=1)


    # Convert the digit data to a color
image
```

```python
    image = (testData[i] *
255).astype("uint8")
    image = cv2.cvtColor(image,
cv2.COLOR_GRAY2RGB)


    # The images are in 28x28 size. Much too
small to see properly
    # So, we resize them to 280x280 for
viewing
    image = cv2.resize(image, (280, 280),
interpolation=cv2.INTER_LINEAR)


    # Add the predicted value on to the
image
    cv2.putText(image, str(prediction[0]),
(20, 40),
                cv2.FONT_HERSHEY_DUPLEX,
1.5, (0, 255, 0), 1)


    # Show the image and prediction
    print("[INFO] Predicted: {}, Actual:
{}".format(
        prediction[0],
np.argmax(testLabels[i])))
    cv2.imshow("Digit", image)
    cv2.waitKey(0)


cv2.destroyAllWindows()
```

Testing the VGG16 model from the Keras applications.

```python
from keras.applications.vgg16 import VGG16
from keras.preprocessing import image
from keras.applications.vgg16 import
preprocess_input, decode_predictions
import numpy as np


model = VGG16(weights='imagenet')


img_path = 'Data/Jellyfish.jpg'
img = image.load_img(img_path,
target_size=(224, 224))
img_data = image.img_to_array(img)
img_data = np.expand_dims(img_data, axis=0)
img_data = preprocess_input(img_data)


preds = model.predict(img_data)


# decode the results into a list of tuples
(class, description, probability)
print('Predicted:',
decode_predictions(preds, top=3)[0])
```

Testing the ResNet50 model from the Keras applications.

```python
from keras.applications.resnet50 import
ResNet50
from keras.preprocessing import image
from keras.applications.resnet50 import
preprocess_input, decode_predictions
import numpy as np


model = ResNet50(weights='imagenet')


img_path = 'Data/Jellyfish.jpg'
img = image.load_img(img_path,
target_size=(224, 224))
x = image.img_to_array(img)
x = np.expand_dims(x, axis=0)
x = preprocess_input(x)


preds = model.predict(x)


# decode the results into a list of tuples
(class, description, probability)
print('Predicted:',
decode_predictions(preds, top=3)[0])
```

The code for the VGG16 model using the Keras Sequential model

```python
from keras.models import Sequential
from keras.layers.core import Flatten,
Dense, Dropout
from keras.layers.convolutional import
Conv2D, MaxPooling2D, ZeroPadding2D
from keras.optimizers import SGD
import numpy as np


def VGG_16(weights_path=None):
    input_shape=(224,224,3)


    model = Sequential()

model.add(ZeroPadding2D((1,1),input_shape=in
put_shape))
    model.add(Conv2D(64, (3, 3),
activation='relu'))
    model.add(ZeroPadding2D((1,1)))
    model.add(Conv2D(64, (3, 3),
activation='relu'))
    model.add(MaxPooling2D((2,2),
strides=(2,2)))

    model.add(ZeroPadding2D((1,1)))
    model.add(Conv2D(128, (3, 3),
activation='relu'))
```

```python
    model.add(ZeroPadding2D((1,1)))
    model.add(Conv2D(128, (3, 3),
activation='relu'))
    model.add(MaxPooling2D((2,2),
strides=(2,2)))

    model.add(ZeroPadding2D((1,1)))
    model.add(Conv2D(256, (3, 3),
activation='relu'))
    model.add(ZeroPadding2D((1,1)))
    model.add(Conv2D(256, (3, 3),
activation='relu'))
    model.add(ZeroPadding2D((1,1)))
    model.add(Conv2D(256, (3, 3),
activation='relu'))
    model.add(MaxPooling2D((2,2),
strides=(2,2)))

    model.add(ZeroPadding2D((1,1)))
    model.add(Conv2D(512, (3, 3),
activation='relu'))
    model.add(ZeroPadding2D((1,1)))
    model.add(Conv2D(512, (3, 3),
activation='relu'))
    model.add(ZeroPadding2D((1,1)))
    model.add(Conv2D(512, (3, 3),
activation='relu'))
```

```
    model.add(MaxPooling2D((2,2),
strides=(2,2)))

    model.add(ZeroPadding2D((1,1)))
    model.add(Conv2D(512, (3, 3),
activation='relu'))
    model.add(ZeroPadding2D((1,1)))
    model.add(Conv2D(512, (3, 3),
activation='relu'))
    model.add(ZeroPadding2D((1,1)))
    model.add(Conv2D(512, (3, 3),
activation='relu'))
    model.add(MaxPooling2D((2,2),
strides=(2,2)))

    model.add(Flatten())
    model.add(Dense(4096,
activation='relu'))
    model.add(Dropout(0.5))
    model.add(Dense(4096,
activation='relu'))
    model.add(Dropout(0.5))
    model.add(Dense(1000,
activation='softmax'))

    if weights_path:
        model.load_weights(weights_path)
```

```
    return model

model = VGG_16()
sgd = SGD(lr=0.1, decay=1e-6, momentum=0.9,
nesterov=True)
model.compile(optimizer=sgd,
loss='categorical_crossentropy')
```

Try transfer learning.

Here, we're building a multi-class image classification system using bottleneck features from the VGG16 pre-trained model in Keras. For the step-by-step guide, head over to the **Using Bottleneck Features for Multi-Class Classification in Keras and TensorFlow** article at **Codes of Interest** (http://www.codesofinterest.com/2017/08/bottleneck-features-multi-class-classification-keras.html).

```
'''
Using Bottleneck Features for Multi-Class
Classification in Keras

We use this technique to build powerful
(high accuracy without overfitting) Image
Classification systems with small
amount of training data.
```

The full tutorial to get this code working
can be found at the "Codes of Interest" Blog
at the following link,
http://www.codesofinterest.com/2017/08/bottl
eneck-features-multi-class-classification-
keras.html

Please go through the tutorial before
attempting to run this code, as it explains
how to setup your training data.

The code was tested on Python 3.5, with the
following library versions,
Keras 2.0.6
TensorFlow 1.2.1
OpenCV 3.2.0

This should work with Theano as well, but
untested.
'''

```python
import numpy as np
from keras.preprocessing.image import
ImageDataGenerator, img_to_array, load_img
from keras.models import Sequential
from keras.layers import Dropout, Flatten,
Dense
from keras import applications
```

```python
from keras.utils.np_utils import
to_categorical
import matplotlib.pyplot as plt
import math
import cv2


# dimensions of our images.
img_width, img_height = 224, 224


top_model_weights_path =
'bottleneck_fc_model.h5'
train_data_dir = 'data/train'
validation_data_dir = 'data/validation'


# number of epochs to train top model
epochs = 50
# batch size used by flow_from_directory and
predict_generator
batch_size = 16



def save_bottlebeck_features():
    # build the VGG16 network
    model =
applications.VGG16(include_top=False,
weights='imagenet')
```

```python
    datagen = ImageDataGenerator(rescale=1.
/ 255)

    generator = datagen.flow_from_directory(
        train_data_dir,
        target_size=(img_width, img_height),
        batch_size=batch_size,
        class_mode=None,
        shuffle=False)

    print(len(generator.filenames))
    print(generator.class_indices)
    print(len(generator.class_indices))

    nb_train_samples =
len(generator.filenames)
    num_classes =
len(generator.class_indices)

    predict_size_train =
int(math.ceil(nb_train_samples /
batch_size))

    bottleneck_features_train =
model.predict_generator(
        generator, predict_size_train)
```

```python
    np.save('bottleneck_features_train.npy',
bottleneck_features_train)


    generator = datagen.flow_from_directory(
        validation_data_dir,
        target_size=(img_width, img_height),
        batch_size=batch_size,
        class_mode=None,
        shuffle=False)


    nb_validation_samples =
len(generator.filenames)


    predict_size_validation = int(
        math.ceil(nb_validation_samples /
batch_size))


    bottleneck_features_validation =
model.predict_generator(
        generator, predict_size_validation)


np.save('bottleneck_features_validation.npy'
,
        bottleneck_features_validation)


def train_top_model():
```

```
    datagen_top =
ImageDataGenerator(rescale=1. / 255)
    generator_top =
datagen_top.flow_from_directory(
        train_data_dir,
        target_size=(img_width, img_height),
        batch_size=batch_size,
        class_mode='categorical',
        shuffle=False)


    nb_train_samples =
len(generator_top.filenames)
    num_classes =
len(generator_top.class_indices)


    # save the class indices to use use
later in predictions
    np.save('class_indices.npy',
generator_top.class_indices)


    # load the bottleneck features saved
earlier
    train_data =
np.load('bottleneck_features_train.npy')


    # get the class lebels for the training
data, in the original order
    train_labels = generator_top.classes
```

```python
    #
https://github.com/fchollet/keras/issues/346
7
    # convert the training labels to
categorical vectors
    train_labels =
to_categorical(train_labels,
num_classes=num_classes)

    generator_top =
datagen_top.flow_from_directory(
        validation_data_dir,
        target_size=(img_width, img_height),
        batch_size=batch_size,
        class_mode=None,
        shuffle=False)

    nb_validation_samples =
len(generator_top.filenames)

    validation_data =
np.load('bottleneck_features_validation.npy'
)

    validation_labels =
generator_top.classes
    validation_labels = to_categorical(
```

```
        validation_labels,
num_classes=num_classes)


    model = Sequential()

model.add(Flatten(input_shape=train_data.sha
pe[1:]))
    model.add(Dense(256, activation='relu'))
    model.add(Dropout(0.5))
    model.add(Dense(num_classes,
activation='sigmoid'))


    model.compile(optimizer='rmsprop',

loss='categorical_crossentropy',
metrics=['accuracy'])


    history = model.fit(train_data,
train_labels,
                        epochs=epochs,

batch_size=batch_size,

validation_data=(validation_data,
validation_labels))


model.save_weights(top_model_weights_path)
```

```python
    (eval_loss, eval_accuracy) =
model.evaluate(
        validation_data, validation_labels,
batch_size=batch_size, verbose=1)

    print("[INFO] accuracy:
{:.2f}%".format(eval_accuracy * 100))
    print("[INFO] Loss:
{}".format(eval_loss))

    plt.figure(1)

    # summarize history for accuracy

    plt.subplot(211)
    plt.plot(history.history['acc'])
    plt.plot(history.history['val_acc'])
    plt.title('model accuracy')
    plt.ylabel('accuracy')
    plt.xlabel('epoch')
    plt.legend(['train', 'test'], loc='upper
left')

    # summarize history for loss

    plt.subplot(212)
    plt.plot(history.history['loss'])
```

```python
    plt.plot(history.history['val_loss'])
    plt.title('model loss')
    plt.ylabel('loss')
    plt.xlabel('epoch')
    plt.legend(['train', 'test'], loc='upper
left')
    plt.show()


def predict():
    # load the class_indices saved in the
earlier step
    class_dictionary =
np.load('class_indices.npy').item()

    num_classes = len(class_dictionary)

    # add the path to your test image below
    image_path = 'path/to/your/test_image'

    orig = cv2.imread(image_path)

    print("[INFO] loading and preprocessing
image...")
    image = load_img(image_path,
target_size=(224, 224))
    image = img_to_array(image)
```

```python
    # important! otherwise the predictions
will be '0'
    image = image / 255

    image = np.expand_dims(image, axis=0)

    # build the VGG16 network
    model =
applications.VGG16(include_top=False,
weights='imagenet')

    # get the bottleneck prediction from the
pre-trained VGG16 model
    bottleneck_prediction =
model.predict(image)

    # build top model
    model = Sequential()

model.add(Flatten(input_shape=bottleneck_pre
diction.shape[1:]))
    model.add(Dense(256, activation='relu'))
    model.add(Dropout(0.5))
    model.add(Dense(num_classes,
activation='sigmoid'))


model.load_weights(top_model_weights_path)
```

```python
    # use the bottleneck prediction on the
top model to get the final
    # classification
    class_predicted =
model.predict_classes(bottleneck_prediction)

    probabilities =
model.predict_proba(bottleneck_prediction)

    inID = class_predicted[0]

    inv_map = {v: k for k, v in
class_dictionary.items()}

    label = inv_map[inID]

    # get the prediction label
    print("Image ID: {}, Label:
{}".format(inID, label))

    # display the predictions with the image
    cv2.putText(orig, "Predicted:
{}".format(label), (10, 30),
                cv2.FONT_HERSHEY_PLAIN, 1.5,
(43, 99, 255), 2)

    cv2.imshow("Classification", orig)
```

```
        cv2.waitKey(0)

        cv2.destroyAllWindows()



save_bottlebeck_features()

train_top_model()

predict()


cv2.destroyAllWindows()
```